TITLES
AND FORMS OF ADDRESS

A GUIDE TO
THEIR CORRECT USE

FOURTEENTH EDITION

ADAM & CHARLES BLACK
LONDON

© 1971 A. AND C. BLACK LTD
4, 5 AND 6 SOHO SQUARE LONDON W1V 6AD

ISBN 0 7136 1266 5

First Edition	.	.	1918
Second Edition	.	.	1929
Third Edition	.	.	1932
Fourth Edition	.	.	1936
Fifth Edition	.	.	1939
Sixth Edition	.	.	1945
Seventh Edition	.	.	1949
Eighth Edition	.	.	1951
Ninth Edition	.	.	1955
Tenth Edition	.	.	1958
Eleventh Edition	.	.	1961
Twelfth Edition	.	.	1964
Thirteenth Edition	.	.	1966
Reprinted	.	.	1969
Fourteenth Edition	.	.	1971
Reprinted	.	.	1972

PRINTED IN GREAT BRITAIN BY
REDWOOD PRESS LIMITED
TROWBRIDGE, WILTSHIRE

INTRODUCTION

THE correct use of titles, and other distinguishing marks of honour or of office, has generally become established over a long period through the usage followed by the title-holders themselves and by those associated with them. Similarly, and very gradually, there occur modifications and changes in practice.

It seems desirable to point out that while great formality may from time to time be appropriate, and the forms to be used in such cases are therefore given, it will more often be proper to use simpler forms, as indicated throughout in this new edition, in ordinary correspondence, whether business or social.

It should be made clear that etiquette is a different subject and is not touched upon in this book.

The publishers are grateful to correspondents who have kindly suggested additions and improvements. At the same time they are bound to say that they are unable to provide an advisory or information service.

1971

CONTENTS

CONTENTS

ABBREVIATIONS

A.A.C.C.A.	.	Associate of the Association of Certified and Corporate Accountants.
A.A.D.C.	.	Air Aide-de-camp.
A.A.F.	.	Auxiliary Air Force (now R.Aux.A.F.).
A.A.G.	.	Assistant-Adjutant-General.
A.A.I.	.	Associate of the Chartered Auctioneers' and Estate-Agents' Institute.
A.B.	.	Bachelor of Arts; able-bodied seaman.
Abp.	.	Archbishop.
A.B.S.	.	Associate Building Societies Institute.
A.C.A.	.	Associate of the Institute of Chartered Accountants.
A.C.C.S.	.	Associate of the Corporation of Secretaries (formerly of Certified Secretaries).
A.C.G.	.	Assistant Chaplain-General.
A.C.G.I.	.	Associate of City and Guilds of London Institute.
A.C.I.A.	.	Associate of the Corporation of Insurance Agents.
A.C.I.B.	.	Associate of the Corporation of Insurance Brokers.
A.C.I.I.	.	Associate of the Chartered Insurance Institute.
A.C.I.S.	.	Associate of the Chartered Institute of Secretaries.
A.C.P.	.	Associate of the College of Preceptors.
A.C.S.	.	Additional Curates Society.
A.C.W.A.	.	Associate of the Institute of Cost and Works Accountants.
A.D.C.	.	Aide-de-camp.
A.D.M.S.	.	Assistant Director of Medical Services.
A.D.O.S.	.	Assistant Director of Ordnance Services.
A.D.V.S.	.	Assistant Director of Veterinary Services.
A.E.A.	.	Atomic Energy Authority; Air Efficiency Award.
A.E.C.	.	Army Educational Corps (now R.A.E.C.).
A.E.R.A.	.	Associate Engraver, Royal Academy.
A.E.U.	.	Amalgamated Engineering Union.
A.F.	.	Admiral of the Fleet.
A.F.A.	.	Amateur Football Alliance.
A.F.A.S.	.	Associate of the Faculty of Architects and Surveyors.
A.F.C.	.	Air Force Cross.
A.F.M.	.	Air Force Medal.
A.F.R.Ae.S.	.	Associate Fellow Royal Aeronautical Society.
A.G.	.	Attorney-General; Adjutant-General.
A.G.I.	.	Artistes Graphiques Internationales; Associate Institute of Certificated Grocers.
A.G.S.M.	.	Associate of the Guildhall School of Music.

I

A.I.A.	. .	Associate Institute of Actuaries; American Institute of Architects.
A.I.A.S.	. .	Associate Surveyor Member of the Incorporated Association of Architects and Surveyors.
A.I.B.	. .	Associate of the Institute of Bankers.
A.I.B.D.	. .	Associate Institute of British Decorators.
A.I.C.S.	. .	Associate of the Institute of Chartered Shipbrokers
A.I.F.	. .	Australian Imperial Forces.
A.I.FireE.	. .	Associate Institution of Fire Engineers.
A.I.H.A.	. .	Associate of Institute of Hospital Almoners.
A.I.I.A.	. .	Associate Insurance Institute of America.
A.I.L.A.	. .	Associate Institute of Landscape Architects.
A.I.M.	. .	Associate Institution of Metallurgists.
A.I.Mar.E.	. .	Associate of the Institute of Marine Engineers.
A.I.M.T.A.	. .	Associate of Institute of Municipal Treasurers and Accountants.
A.Inst.P.	. .	Associate of the Institute of Physics.
A.K.C.	. .	Associate of King's College, London.
A.L.A.	. .	Associate of the Library Association.
A.L.C.D.	. .	Associate London College of Divinity.
A.L.C.M.	. .	Associate of the London College of Music.
A.L.I.	. .	Argyll Light Infantry.
A.L.S.	. .	Associate of the Linnean Society.
A.M.	. .	Master of Arts; Albert Medal; Alpes Maritimes.
A.M.A.	. .	Assistant Masters' Association; Australian Medical Association; Associate Museums Association.
A.M.G.O.T.	.	Allied Military Government of Occupied Territory.
A.M.I.Fire E.	.	Associate Member Institution of Fire Engineers.
A.N.A.	.	Associate National Academician (America).
Anon.	. .	Anonymously.
ANZAC	.	Australian and New Zealand Army Corps.
A.O.A.	. .	Air Officer in Charge of Administration.
A.O.C.	.	Air Officer Commanding.
A.O.C.-in-C.	.	Air Officer Commanding-in-Chief.
A.O.D.	.	Army Ordnance Department.
A.P.I.	. .	Associate of Plastics Institute.
A.P.T.C.	.	Army Physical Training Corps.
A.Q.M.G.	.	Assistant-Quartermaster-General.
A.R.A.	.	Associate Royal Academy.
A.R.A.D.	.	Associate of the Royal Academy of Dancing.
A.R.A.M.	.	Associate Royal Academy of Music.
A.R.B.S.	.	Associate Royal Society of British Sculptors.
A.R.C.A.	.	Associate Royal College of Art; Associate Royal Canadian Academy.
A.R.Cam.A.	.	Associate Royal Cambrian Academy.

A.R.C.E.	. .	Academical Rank of Civil Engineers.
A.R.C.M.	. .	Associate of the Royal College of Music.
A.R.C.O.	. .	Associate Royal College of Organists.
A.R.C.S.	. .	Associate Royal College of Science.
A.R.E.	. .	Associate Royal Society of Painter-Etchers and Engravers.
A.R.I.B.A.	. .	Associate Royal Institute of British Architects.
A.R.I.C.	. .	Associate Royal Institute of Chemistry.
A.R.I.C.S.	. .	Professional Associate Royal Institution of Chartered Surveyors.
A.R.M.S.	. .	Associate Royal Society of Miniature Painters.
A.R.P.	. .	Air Raid Precautions.
A.R.P.S.	. .	Associate Royal Photographic Society.
A.R.R.C.	. .	Associate Royal Red Cross.
A.R.S.A.	. .	Associate Royal Scottish Academy.
A.R.S.L.	. .	Associate of the Royal Society of Literature.
A.R.S.M.	. .	Associate Royal School of Mines.
A.R.V.A.	. .	Associate Rating and Valuation Association.
A.R.W.A.	. .	Associate Royal West of England Academy.
A.R.W.S.	. .	Associate Royal Society of Painters in Water Colours.
A.S.A.A.	. .	Associate Society of Incorporated Accountants and Auditors.
A.S.A.M.	. .	Associate Society of Art Masters.
A.S.L.I.B.	. .	Association of Special Libraries and Information Bureaux.
Ass. Com. Gen.	.	Assistant-Commissary-General.
Assoc. Sc.	. .	Associate in Science.
A.T.C.	. .	Air Training Corps.
A.T.C.L.	. .	Associate of Trinity College of Music, London.
A.T.S.	. .	Auxiliary Territorial Service (now W.R.A.C.).
A.V.D.	. .	Army Veterinary Department.
B.A.	. .	Bachelor of Arts.
B.A.O.	. .	Bachelor of Obstetrics.
B.A.O.R.	. .	British Army of the Rhine.
B.A.S.	. .	Bachelor in Agricultural Science.
B.B.C.	. .	British Broadcasting Corporation.
B.C.	. .	Before Christ; British Columbia.
B.C.E.	. .	Bachelor of Civil Engineering.
B.Chir.	. .	Bachelor of Surgery.
B.C.L.	. .	Bachelor of Civil Law.
B.D.	. .	Bachelor of Divinity.
B.Ed.	. .	Bachelor of Education.
B.E.M.	. .	British Empire Medal.

B.Eng.	. .	Bachelor of Engineering.
B.I.F. .	. .	British Industries Fair.
B.Litt. .	. .	Bachelor of Letters.
B.LL. .	. .	Bachelor of Laws.
B.M. .	. .	Bachelor of Medicine, Oxford University.
B.M.A.	. .	British Medical Association.
B.Mus.	. .	Bachelor of Music.
B.O.A.C.	. .	British Overseas Airways Corporation.
Bp. .	. .	Bishop.
B.Phil.	. .	Bachelor of Philosophy.
B.R.C.S.	. .	British Red Cross Society.
B.S. .	. .	Bachelor of Surgery.
B.Sc. .	. .	Bachelor of Science.
Bt. .	. .	Baronet.
B.Th. .	. .	Bachelor of Theology.
C.A. .	. .	County Alderman; Chartered Accountant (Scotland and Canada).
Cantab.	. .	Of Cambridge University.
Cantuar.	. .	(Archbishop of) Canterbury.
Carliol.	. .	(Bishop of) Carlisle.
C.A.S. .	. .	Chief of the Air Staff.
C.B. .	. .	Companion of the Bath.
C.B.C. .	. .	Canadian Broadcasting Corporation.
C.B.E. .	. .	Commander of the Order of the British Empire.
C.B.I. .	. .	Confederation of British Industry.
C.B.S.A.	. .	Clay Bird Shooting Association.
C.C. .	. .	Companion of the Order of Canada; County Council; Cricket Club; Cycling Club; County Court.
C.D. .	. .	Canadian Decoration; Civil Defence.
C.E. .	. .	Civil Engineer.
C.Eng.	. .	Chartered Engineer.
C.E.T.S.	. .	Church of England Temperance Society.
C.F. .	. .	Chaplain to the Forces.
C.G.M.	. .	Conspicuous Gallantry Medal.
C.G.S. .	. .	Chief of the General Staff.
C.H. .	. .	Companion of Honour.
Ch.B. .	. .	Bachelor of Surgery.
Ch.M. .	. .	Master of Surgery.
C.I. .	. .	Imperial Order of the Crown of India; Channel Islands.
Cicestr.	. .	(Bishop of) Chichester.
C.I.D. .	. .	Criminal Investigation Department.
C.I.E. .	. .	Companion of the Order of the Indian Empire.
C.I.G.S.	. .	Chief of the Imperial General Staff (now C.G.S.).

C.I.Mech.E.	.	Companion of the Institution of Mechanical Engineers.
C.-in-C.	.	Commander-in-Chief.
C.I.V.	.	City Imperial Volunteers.
C.J.	.	Chief Justice.
C.L.	.	Commander of Order of Leopold.
C.M.	.	Medal of Courage (Canada); Master in Surgery; Certificated Master.
C.M.G.	.	Companion of St. Michael and St. George.
C.M.S.	.	Church Missionary Society.
C.O.	.	Commanding Officer; Colonial Office; Conscientious Objector.
Col.-Sergt.	.	Colour-Sergeant.
Comdr.	.	Commander.
Comdt.	.	Commandant.
Comr.	.	Commissioner.
Corr. Mem. or Fell.		Corresponding Member or Fellow.
C.O.S.	.	Charity Organization Society.
C.P.A.	.	Chartered Patent Agent.
Cpl.	.	Corporal.
C.P.R.	.	Canadian Pacific Railway.
C.P.R.E.	.	Council for the Preservation of Rural England.
C.Q.M.S.	.	Company Quartermaster-Sergeant.
C.R.	.	Community of the Resurrection.
C.S.	.	Civil Service.
C.S.C.	.	Conspicuous Service Cross.
C.S.I.	.	Companion of the Order of the Star of India.
C.S.M.	.	Company Sergeant-Major.
C.SS.R.	.	Congregation of the Most Holy Redeemer (Redemptorist Order).
C.U.	.	Cambridge University.
C.U.A.C.	.	Cambridge University Athletic Club.
C.U.A.F.C.	.	Cambridge University Association Football Club.
C.U.B.C.	.	Cambridge University Boat Club.
C.U.C.C.	.	Cambridge University Cricket Club.
C.U.R.U.F.C.	.	Cambridge University Rugby Union Football Club.
C.V.O.	.	Commander of the Royal Victorian Order.
D.A.A.G.	.	Deputy-Assistant-Adjutant-General.
D.A.C.G.	.	Deputy Assistant Chaplain-General.
D.A.D.O.S.	.	Deputy Assistant Director of Ordnance Services.
D.A.D.Q.	.	Deputy Assistant Director of Quartering.
D.A.G.	.	Deputy-Adjutant-General.
D.A.Q.M.G.	.	Deputy-Assistant-Quartermaster-General.
D.A.R.	.	Daughters of the American Revolution.
D.B.E.	.	Dame Commander Order of the British Empire.

D.C.B.	. .	Dame Commander of the Bath.
D.C.H.	. .	Diploma in Child Health.
D.C.L.	. .	Doctor of Civil Law.
D.C.M.	. .	Distinguished Conduct Medal.
D.C.M.G.	. .	Dame Commander of St. Michael and St. George.
D.C.T.	. .	Doctor of Christian Theology.
D.C.V.O.	. .	Dame Commander of the Royal Victorian Order.
D.D.	. .	Doctor of Divinity.
D.D.M.S.	. .	Deputy Director of Medical Services.
D.D.S.	. .	Doctor of Dental Surgery; Director of Dental Services.
D.Eng.	. .	Doctor of Engineering.
D.F.C.	. .	Distinguished Flying Cross.
D.G.	. .	*Dei Gratia* (by the grace of God); Dragoon Guards.
D.G.M.S.	. .	Director-General of Medical Services.
D.G.M.W.	. .	Director-General of Military Works.
D.L.	. .	Deputy Lieutenant.
D.L.I.	. .	Durham Light Infantry.
D.Litt. or D.Lit.	. .	Doctor of Literature; Doctor of Letters.
D.M.	. .	Doctor of Medicine, Oxford University.
D.M.R.E.	. .	Diploma in Medical Radiology and Electrology.
D.M.S.	. .	Director of Medical Services.
D.Obst. R.C.O.G.	. .	Diploma Royal College of Obstetricians and Gynaecologists.
Doc. Eng.	. .	Doctor of Engineering.
D.O.M.	. .	*Deo Optimo Maximo* (to God the best and greatest).
D.O.S.	. .	Director of Ordnance Services.
D.P.H.	. .	Diploma in Public Health.
D.Phil.	. .	Doctor of Philosophy, Oxford University.
Dr.	. .	Doctor; Debtor.
D.S.C.	. .	Distinguished Service Cross.
D.Sc.	. .	Doctor of Science.
D.S.M.	. .	Distinguished Service Medal.
D.S.O.	. .	Companion of the Distinguished Service Order.
D.Theol.	. .	Doctor of Theology.
Dunelm.	. .	(Bishop of) Durham.
Ebor.	. .	(Archbishop of) York.
E.D.	. .	Efficiency Decoration.
E.E.C.	. .	European Economic Community.
E.F.T.A.	. .	European Free Trade Association.
E.G.M.	. .	Empire Gallantry Medal.
E.I.	. .	East Indian; East Indies.
E.I.C.S.	. .	East India Company's Service.
E.N.S.A.	. .	Entertainments National Service Association.

E.R.	. . .	*Edwardus Rex* (King Edward), also *Elizabetha Regina* (Queen Elizabeth).
E.R.D.	. .	Emergency Reserve Decoration (Army).
F.A.	. .	Football Association.
F.A.A.	. .	Fleet Air Arm.
F.A.C.C.A.	. .	Fellow of the Association of Certified and Corporate Accountants.
F.A.C.S.	. .	Fellow American College of Surgeons.
F.A.G.S.	. .	Fellow American Geographical Society.
F.A.I.	. .	Fellow of the Chartered Auctioneers' and Estate Agents' Institute.
F.A.I.A.	. .	Fellow of the Association of International Accountants.
F.A.I.I.	. .	Fellow Australian Insurance Institute.
F.A.L.P.A.	. .	Fellow Incorporated Society Auctioneers and Landed Property Agents.
F.A.N.Y.	. .	First Aid Nursing Yeomanry.
F.A.O.	. .	Food and Agriculture Organization.
F.A.S.	. .	Fellow Antiquarian Society.
F.B.A.	. .	Fellow British Academy.
F.B.A.A.	. .	Fellow of the British Association of Accountants and Auditors.
F.B.I.	. .	Federation of British Industries (now C.B.I.); Federal Bureau of Investigation (U.S.A.).
F.B.I.M.	. .	Fellow British Institute of Management.
F.B.O.A.	. .	Fellow British Optical Association.
F.B.O.U.	. .	Fellow British Ornithologists' Union.
F.B.S.	. .	Fellow Building Societies Institute.
F.B.S.E.	. .	Fellow Botanical Society, Edinburgh.
F.C.A.	. .	Fellow Institute of Chartered Accountants.
F.C.C.S.	. .	Fellow Corporation of Secretaries (formerly of Certified Secretaries).
F.C.G.I.	. .	Fellow City and Guilds of London Institute.
F.C.I.A.	. .	Fellow Corporation of Insurance Agents.
F.C.I.P.A.	. .	Fellow Chartered Institute of Patent Agents.
F.C.I.B.	. .	Fellow Corporation of Insurance Brokers.
F.C.I.I.	. .	Fellow Chartered Insurance Institute.
F.C.I.S.	. .	Fellow Chartered Institute of Secretaries.
F.C.I.T.	. .	Fellow Chartered Institute of Transport.
F.C.O.	. .	Foreign and Commonwealth Office.
F.C.P.	. .	Fellow College of Preceptors.
F.C.S.	. .	Fellow Chemical Society.
F.C.T.B.	. .	Fellow College of Teachers of the Blind.
F.C.W.A.	. .	Fellow Institute of Cost and Works Accountants.
F.E.I.S.	. .	Fellow Educational Institute of Scotland.

F.E.S.	. .	Fellow Entomological Society; Fellow Ethnological Society.
F.F.A.	. .	Fellow Faculty of Actuaries.
F.F.A.S.	. .	Fellow Faculty of Architects and Surveyors.
F.G.I.	. .	Fellow Institute of Certificated Grocers.
F.G.O.	. .	Fellow Guild of Organists.
F.G.S.	. .	Fellow Geological Society.
F.H.A.S.	. .	Fellow Highland and Agricultural Society of Scotland.
F.I.A.	. .	Fellow Institute of Actuaries.
F.I.A.A. & S.	.	Fellow Incorporated Association of Architects and Surveyors.
F.I.Arb.	. .	Fellow Institute of Arbitrators.
F.I.B.	. .	Fellow of the Institute of Bankers.
F.I.B.D.	. .	Fellow Institute of British Decorators.
F.I.C.E.	. .	Fellow Institution of Civil Engineers.
F.I.C.S.	. .	Fellow Institute of Chartered Shipbrokers; Fellow International College of Surgeons.
F.I.E.E.	. .	Fellow Institution of Electrical Engineers.
F.I.E.R.E.	. .	Fellow Institution of Electronic & Radio Engineers.
F.Illum.E.S.	. .	Fellow Illuminating Engineering Society.
F.I.GasE.	. .	Fellow Institution of Gas Engineers.
F.I.H.	. .	Fellow Institute of Hygiene.
F.I.H.E.	. .	Fellow Institution of Highway Engineers.
F.I.H.V.E.	. .	Fellow Institution of Heating & Ventilating Engineers.
F.I.Inst.	. .	Fellow Imperial Institute.
F.I.L.	. .	Fellow Institute of Linguists.
F.I.M.	. .	Fellow Institution of Metallurgists.
F.I.MechE.	. .	Fellow Institution of Mechanical Engineers.
F.I.M.I.	. .	Fellow Institute of the Motor Industry.
F.I.Min.E.	. .	Fellow Institution of Mining Engineers.
F.I.M.T.A.	. .	Fellow of Institute of Municipal Treasurers and Accountants.
F.I.Mun.E.	. .	Fellow Institution of Municipal Engineers.
F.Inst.D.	. .	Fellow Institute of Directors.
F.Inst.F.	. .	Fellow Institute of Fuel.
F.Inst.Met.	. .	Fellow Institute of Metals.
F.Inst.P.	. .	Fellow Institute of Physics.
F.Inst.P.I.	. .	Fellow Institute of Patentees (Incorporated).
F.I.O.	. .	Fellow Institute of Ophthalmic Opticians.
F.I.O.B.	. .	Fellow Institute of Builders.
F.I.P.R.	. .	Fellow of the Institute of Public Relations.
F.I.Prod.E.	. .	Fellow Institution of Production Engineers.
F.I.S.A.	. .	Fellow Incorporated Secretaries' Association.
F.I.S.E.	. .	Fellow Institution of Sanitary Engineers.

F.I.Struct.E.	.	Fellow Institution of Structural Engineers.
F.J.I.	.	Fellow Institute of Journalists.
F.K.C.	.	Fellow King's College, London.
F.L.A.	.	Fellow Library Association.
F.L.A.S.	.	Fellow Chartered Land Agents' Society.
F.L.G.A.	.	Fellow Local Government Association.
F.L.S.	.	Fellow Linnean Society.
F.M.	.	Field-Marshal.
F.O.	.	Foreign Office; Field Officer; Flying Officer.
F.Ph.S.	.	Fellow of the Philosophical Society of England.
F.Phys.S.	.	Fellow Physical Society.
F.P.I.	.	Fellow Plastics Institute.
F.R.A.D.	.	Fellow of the Royal Academy of Dancing.
F.R.Ae.S.	.	Fellow Royal Aeronautical Society.
F.R.A.I.	.	Fellow Royal Anthropological Institute.
F.R.A.M.	.	Fellow Royal Academy of Music.
F.R.A.S.	.	Fellow Royal Astronomical Society; Fellow Royal Asiatic Society.
F.R.B.S.	.	Fellow Royal Botanic Society; Fellow Royal Society of British Sculptors.
F.R.C.M.	.	Fellow Royal College of Music.
F.R.C.O.	.	Fellow Royal College of Organists.
F.R.C.O.G.	.	Fellow of the Royal College of Obstetricians and Gynaecologists.
F.R.C.P.	.	Fellow Royal College of Physicians.
F.R.C.P.E.	.	Fellow Royal College of Physicians of Edinburgh.
F.R.C.P.Glas.	.	Fellow of Royal College of Physicians and Surgeons, Glasgow.
F.R.C.P.I.	.	Fellow Royal College of Physicians in Ireland.
F.R.C.S.	.	Fellow Royal College of Surgeons.
F.R.C.S.E.	.	Fellow Royal College of Surgeons of Edinburgh.
F.R.C.S.Glas.	.	Fellow of Royal College of Surgeons, Glasgow.
F.R.C.S.I.	.	Fellow Royal College of Surgeons in Ireland.
F.R.C.V.S.	.	Fellow Royal College of Veterinary Surgeons.
F.R.Econ.S.	.	Fellow Royal Economic Society.
F.R.E.S.	.	Fellow Royal Entomological Society of London.
F.R.F.P.S.G.	.	Fellow Royal Faculty of Physicians and Surgeons Glasgow (now F.R.C.P.Glas.).
F.R.G.S.	.	Fellow Royal Geographical Society.
F.R.Hist.S.	.	Fellow Royal Historical Society.
F.R.H.S.	.	Fellow Royal Horticultural Society.
F.R.I.	.	Fellow Royal Institution.
F.R.I.B.A.	.	Fellow Royal Institute of British Architects.
F.R.I.C.	.	Fellow Royal Institute of Chemistry.
F.R.I.C.S.	.	Fellow Royal Institution of Chartered Surveyors.
F.R.I.N.A.	.	Fellow Royal Institution of Naval Architects.

F.R.Met.S.	. .	Fellow Royal Meteorological Society.
F.R.M.S.	. .	Fellow Royal Microscopical Society.
F.R.N.S.A.	. .	Fellow Royal School of Naval Architecture.
F.R.P.S.	. .	Fellow Royal Photographic Society.
F.R.P.S.L.	. .	Fellow Royal Philatelic Society, London.
F.R.S.	. .	Fellow Royal Society.
F.R.S.A.	. .	Fellow Royal Society of Arts.
F.R.S.A.I.	. .	Fellow Royal Society of Antiquaries of Ireland.
F.R.San.I.	. .	Fellow Royal Sanitary Institute (now F.R.S.H.).
F.R.S.C.	. .	Fellow Royal Society of Canada.
F.R.S.E.	. .	Fellow Royal Society of Edinburgh.
F.R.S.G.S.	. .	Fellow Royal Scottish Geographical Society.
F.R.S.H.	. .	Fellow Royal Society for the Promotion of Health (formerly F.R.San.I.).
F.R.S.L.	. .	Fellow Royal Society of Literature.
F.R.U.I.	. .	Fellow Royal University of Ireland.
F.R.V.A.	. .	Fellow Rating and Valuation Association.
F.R.Z.S.Scot.	.	Fellow of the Royal Zoological Society of Scotland.
F.S.A.	. .	Fellow Society of Antiquaries.
F.S.A.A.	. .	Fellow Society of Incorporated Accountants and Auditors.
F.S.A.Scot.	. .	Fellow Society of Antiquaries of Scotland.
F.S.I.A.	. .	Fellow Society of Industrial Artists.
F.S.M.C.	. .	Freeman Spectacle Makers' Company.
F.S.S.	. .	Fellow Royal Statistical Society.
F.T.C.D.	. .	Fellow Trinity College, Dublin.
F.T.C.L.	. .	Fellow Trinity College of Music, London.
F.T.I.	. .	Fellow Textile Institute.
F.Z.S.	. .	Fellow Zoological Society.
F.Z.S.Scot.	. .	Fellow Zoological Society of Scotland (now F.R.Z.S.Scot.).
G.A.T.T.	. .	General Agreement on Tariffs and Trade.
G.B.E.	. .	Knight (or Dame) Grand Cross Order of the British Empire.
G.C.	. .	George Cross.
G.C.B.	. .	Knight (or Dame) Grand Cross of the Bath.
G.C.H.	. .	Knight Grand Cross of Hanover.
G.C.I.E.	. .	Knight Grand Commander of the Indian Empire.
G.C.M.G.	. .	Knight (or Dame) Grand Cross of St. Michael and St. George.
G.C.S.I.	. .	Knight Grand Commander of the Star of India.
G.C.V.O.	. .	Knight (or Dame) Grand Cross of the Royal Victorian Order.
G.L.C.	. .	Greater London Council.
G.M.	. .	George Medal.

G.M.C.	.	.	General Medical Council.
G.O.C.	.	.	General Officer Commanding.
G.O.C.-in-C.	.	.	General Officer Commanding-in-Chief.
G.P.	.	.	General Practitioner.
G.Ph.	.	.	Graduate in Pharmacy.
G.R.	.	.	*Georgius Rex* (King George).
Grad.I.A.E.		.	Graduate Institution of Automobile Engineers.
G.R.C.M.	.	.	Graduate Royal College of Music.
G.R.S.M.	.	.	Graduate Royal School of Music.

H.A.C.	.	.	Honourable Artillery Company.
H.B.M.	.	.	His (or Her) Britannic Majesty.
H.E.	.	.	His Excellency; His Eminence.
H.E.H.	.	.	His (or Her) Exalted Highness.
H.E.I.C.	.	.	Honourable East India Company.
H.E.I.C.S.	.	.	Honourable East India Company's Service.
H.F.R.A.	.	.	Honorary Foreign Member of the Royal Academy.
H.G.	.	.	Home Guard.
H.H.	.	.	His (or Her) Highness; His Holiness.
H.I.H.	.	.	His (or Her) Imperial Highness.
H.I.M.	.	.	His (or Her) Imperial Majesty.
H.L.I.	.	.	Highland Light Infantry.
H.M.	.	.	His (or Her) Majesty; His (or Her) Majesty's.
H.M.A.S.	.	.	His (or Her) Majesty's Australian Ship.
H.M.C.S.	.	.	His (or Her) Majesty's Canadian Ship.
H.M.I.	.	.	His (or Her) Majesty's Inspector.
H.M.L.	.	.	Her Majesty's Lieutenant.
H.M.S.	.	.	His (or Her) Majesty's Ship.
H.M.S.O.	.	.	His (or Her) Majesty's Stationery Office.
Hon.	.	.	Honourable; honorary.
Hon.F.R.A.M.		.	Honorary Fellow Royal Academy of Music.
Hon.R.A.M.		.	Honorary Member Royal Academy of Music.
H.R.A.	.	.	Honorary Royal Academician.
H.R.C.A.	.	.	Honorary Member Royal Cambrian Academy.
H.R.H.	.	.	His (or Her) Royal Highness.
H.R.H.A.	.	.	Honorary Member of Royal Hibernian Academy.
H.R.S.A.	.	.	Honorary Member of Royal Scottish Academy.
H.S.H.	.	.	His (or Her) Serene Highness.

I.A.	.	.	Indian Army.
I.A.T.A.	.	.	International Air Transport Association.
I.British E.	.	.	Institute of British Engineers.
I.C.A.A.	.	.	Invalid Children's Aid Association.
I.C.E.	.	.	Institution of Civil Engineers.
I.C.I.	.	.	Imperial Chemical Industries.
I.C.R.C.	.	.	International Committee of the Red Cross.

I.C.S.	.	.	Indian Civil Service.
I.E.E.	.	.	Institution of Electrical Engineers.
I.F.S.	.	.	Irish Free State.
I.H.S.	.	.	*Jesus Hominum Salvator* (Jesus the Saviour of Men), more correctly IHΣ, the first three letters of the name of Jesus in Greek.
I.H.V.E.	.	.	Institution of Heating and Ventilating Engineers.
I.L.O.	.	.	International Labour Office.
I.L.P.	.	.	Independent Labour Party.
I.M.A.	.	.	International Music Association.
I.M.E.A.	.	.	Incorporated Municipal Electrical Association.
I.Mech.E.	.	.	Institution of Mechanical Engineers.
I.Min.E.	.	.	Institution of Mining Engineers.
Inst.Act.	.	.	Institute of Actuaries.
Inst.D.	.	.	Institute of Directors.
Inst.F.	.	.	Institute of Fuel.
Inst.Met.	.	.	Institute of Metals.
I.O.G.T.	.	.	International Order of Good Templars.
I.O.O.F.	.	.	Independent Order of Oddfellows.
I.O.P.	.	.	Institute Painters in Oil Colours.
I.S.C.	.	.	Indian Staff Corps.
I.S.M.	.	.	Imperial Service Medal.
I.S.O.	.	.	Imperial Service Order.
I.T.A.	.	.	Independent Television Authority.
J.	.	.	Judge; Justice.
J.A.	.	.	Judge Advocate.
J.A.G.	.	.	Judge Advocate General.
J.D.	.	.	Doctor of Jurisprudence.
J.P.	.	.	Justice of the Peace.
J.T.C.	.	.	Junior Training Corps.
K.A.R.	.	.	King's African Rifles.
K.B.E.	.	.	Knight Commander Order of the British Empire.
K.C.	.	.	King's Counsel.
K.C.B.	.	.	Knight Commander of the Bath.
K.C.C.	.	.	Commander of Order of Crown, Belgian and Congo Free State.
K.C.H.	.	.	Knight Commander of Hanover.
K.C.I.E.	.	.	Knight Commander of the Indian Empire.
K.C.L.	.	.	King's College, London.
K.C.M.G.	.	.	Knight Commander of St. Michael and St. George.
K.C.S.I.	.	.	Knight Commander of the Star of India.
K.C.V.O.	.	.	Knight Commander of the Royal Victorian Order
K.E.H.	.	.	King Edward's Horse.
K.G.	.	.	Knight of the Order of the Garter.

K.G.F.	. .	Knight of the Golden Fleece.
K.H. .	. .	Knight of Hanover.
K.H.C.	. .	Honorary Chaplain to the King.
K.H.P.	. .	Honorary Physician to the King.
K.H.S.	. .	Honorary Surgeon to the King; Knight of the Holy Sepulchre.
K.i.H. .	. .	Kaisar-i-Hind Medal.
K.M. .	. .	Knight of Malta.
K.O.R.R.	. .	King's Own Royal Regiment.
K.O.S.B.	. .	King's Own Scottish Borderers.
K.O.Y.L.I. .	. .	King's Own Yorkshire Light Infantry.
K.P. .	. .	Knight of the Order of St. Patrick.
K.P.M.	. .	King's Police Medal.
K.R.C.	. .	Knight of the Red Cross.
K.R.R.	. .	King's Royal Rifles.
K.R.R.C.	. .	King's Royal Rifle Corps.
K.S. .	. .	King's Scholar.
K.S.G.	. .	Knight of St. Gregory.
K.S.L.I.	. .	King's Shropshire Light Infantry.
K.T. .	. .	Knight of the Order of the Thistle.
Kt. or Knt. .	.	Knight.
L.A.C.	.	Leading Aircraftman; London Athletic Club.
L.A.H. (Dublin)	.	Licentiate of Apothecaries' Hall, Dublin.
L.A.M.	.	London Academy of Music.
L.C.C. .	.	London County Council.
L.Ch. .	.	Licentiate in Surgery.
L.C.J. .	.	Lord Chief Justice.
L.C.P. .	.	Licentiate of the College of Preceptors.
L.Div. .	.	Licentiate in Divinity.
L.D.S. .	.	Licentiate in Dental Surgery.
L.E.A. .	.	Local Education Authority.
L.G.U.	.	Ladies' Golf Union.
L.H.D.	.	(*Literarum Humaniorum Doctor*) Doctor of Literature.
L.I. .	.	Light Infantry; Long Island.
Lic.Med.	.	Licentiate in Medicine.
Lit. .	.	Literature; Literary.
Lit.D. .	.	Doctor of Literature.
Lit.Hum.	.	(*Literæ Humaniores*) Classics.
Litt.D.	.	Doctor of Literature.
L.J. .	.	Lord Justice.
L.L.A. .	.	Lady Literate in Arts.
LL.B. .	.	Bachelor of Laws.
LL.D. .	.	Doctor of Laws.
LL.M. .	.	Master of Laws.
L.M. .	. .	Licentiate in Midwifery.

L.M.S.S.A.	. .	Licentiate in Medicine and Surgery, Society of Apothecaries, London.
L.P.T.B.	. .	London Passenger Transport Board.
L.R.A.D.	. .	Licentiate of the Royal Academy of Dancing.
L.R.A.M.	. .	Licentiate Royal Academy of Music.
L.R.C.M.	. .	Licentiate Royal College of Music.
L.R.C.P.	. .	Licentiate Royal College of Physicians.
L.R.C.P.E.	. .	Licentiate Royal College of Physicians, Edinburgh.
L.R.C.P.I.	. .	Licentiate Royal College of Physicians, Ireland.
L.R.C.S.	. .	Licentiate Royal College of Surgeons.
L.R.C.S.E.	. .	Licentiate Royal College of Surgeons, Edinburgh.
L.R.C.S.I.	. .	Licentiate Royal College of Surgeons, Ireland.
L.R.C.V.S.	. .	Licentiate Royal College of Veterinary Surgeons.
L.R.I.B.A.	. .	Licentiate Royal Institute of British Architects.
L.S.A.	. .	Licentiate Society of Apothecaries.
L.S.O.	. .	London Symphony Orchestra.
L.T.C.L.	. .	Licentiate Trinity College of Music, London.
Lt.-Col.	. .	Lieutenant-Colonel.
Lt.-Gen.	. .	Lieutenant-General.
L.Th.	. .	Licentiate in Theology.
L.T.M.	. .	Licentiate in Tropical Medicine.
M.	. .	Marquess; Member; Monsieur.
M.A.	. .	Master of Arts.
M.A.B.	. .	Metropolitan Asylums Board.
M.A.I.	. .	Master of Engineering (*Magister in Arte Ingeniaria*).
M.A.O.	. .	Master of Obstetric Art.
M.A.Sc.	. .	Master of Applied Science.
M.B.	. .	Bachelor of Medicine.
M.B.E.	. .	Member Order of the British Empire.
M.B.I.M.	. .	Member British Institute of Management.
M.B.O.U.	. .	Member British Ornithologists' Union.
M.C.	. .	Military Cross; Master of Ceremonies.
M.C.C.	. .	Marylebone Cricket Club.
M.Ch.	. .	Master in Surgery.
M.Ch.D.	. .	Master in Dental Surgery.
M.Ch.Orth.	. .	Master in Orthopaedic Surgery.
M.C.L.	. .	Master of Civil Law.
M.C.M.E.S.	. .	Member Civil and Mechanical Engineers' Society.
M.Com.	. .	Master of Commerce.
M.C.S.	. .	Malayan Civil Service.
M.D.	. .	Doctor of Medicine.
M.D.S.	. .	Master in Dental Surgery.
M.E.C.	. .	Member Executive Council.
M.E.F.	. .	Middle East Force.
M.E.I.C.	. .	Member Engineering Institute of Canada.

M.Eng.	. .	Master of Engineering.
M.F.H.	. .	Master of Foxhounds.
M.G.I.	. .	Member Institute of Certificated Grocers.
Mgr. .	. .	Monsignor.
M.H.A.	. .	Member of House of Assembly.
M.H.K.	. .	Member of the House of Keys.
M.H.R.	. .	Member House of Representatives.
M.Hy. .	. .	Master of Hygiene.
M.I. .	. .	Military Intelligence.
M.I.A.	. .	Member of the Institute of Arbitrators.
M.I.A.A.	. .	Member of the Institute of Automobile Assessors.
M.I.British E.	.	Member Institute of British Engineers.
M.I.C.E.	. .	Member Institution of Civil Engineers.
M.I.Chem.E.	.	Member Institution of Chemical Engineers.
M.I.E.E.	. .	Member Institution of Electrical Engineers.
M.I.Fire E. .	.	Member Institution of Fire Engineers.
M.I.Gas E. .	.	Member Institution of Gas Engineers.
M.I.Mar.E. .	.	Member Institute of Marine Engineers.
M.I.Mech.E.	.	Member Institution of Mechanical Engineers.
M.I.Min.E. .	.	Member Institution of Mining Engineers.
M.I.M.M. .	.	Member Institution of Mining and Metallurgy.
M.I.Mun.E. .	.	Member Institution of Municipal Engineers.
M.Inst.Met. .	.	Member Institute of Metals.
M.Inst.Pet. .	.	Member Institute of Petroleum.
M.Inst.R.A. .	.	Member Institute of Registered Architects.
M.I.O.B.	. .	Member Institute of Builders.
M.I.P.R.	. .	Member of the Institute of Public Relations.
M.I.Prod.E. .	.	Member Institution of Production Engineers.
M.I.Struct.E.	.	Member Institution Structural Engineers.
M.I.T.M.A. .	.	Member Institute of Trade Mark Agents.
M.I.W.E.	. .	Member Institution of Water Engineers.
M.J.I. .	. .	Member Institute of Journalists.
M.J.S. .	. .	Member Japan Society.
M.K.W.	. .	Military Knight of Windsor.
M.L. .	. .	Licentiate in Medicine; Master of Laws.
M.L.A.	. .	Member Legislative Assembly.
M.L.C..	. .	Member Legislative Council.
Mlle. .	. .	*Mademoiselle* (Miss).
M.L.S.B.	. .	Member London School Board.
M.L.S.C.	. .	Member London Society of Compositors.
M.M. .	. .	Military Medal.
Mme. .	. .	Madame.
Mods. .	. .	Moderations (Oxford).
M.O.H.	. .	Medical Officer of Health; Master of Otter Hounds.
M.O.I..	. .	Ministry of Information.

Most Revd. . .	Most Reverend (of an Archbishop and Bishop of Meath).
M.P. . .	Member of Parliament.
M.P.C. .	Member of Parliament, Canada.
M.P.P. .	Member of Provincial Parliament.
M.P.S. . .	Member Pharmaceutical Society; Member Philological Society; Member Physical Society.
M.R. . .	Master of the Rolls.
M.R.A.S. .	Member Royal Asiatic Society; Member Royal Academy of Science.
M.R.C. .	Medical Research Council.
M.R.C.C. .	Member Royal College of Chemistry.
M.R.C.O. .	Member Royal College of Organists.
M.R.C.O.G. .	Member of Royal College of Obstetricians and Gynaecologists.
M.R.C.P. .	Member Royal College of Physicians.
M.R.C.P.E. .	Member Royal College of Physicians, Edinburgh.
M.R.C.P.I. .	Member Royal College of Physicians, Ireland.
M.R.C.S. .	Member Royal College of Surgeons.
M.R.C.V.S. .	Member Royal College of Veterinary Surgeons.
M.R.I. .	Member Royal Institution.
M.R.I.A. .	Member Royal Irish Academy.
M.R.I.N.A. .	Member Royal Institution of Naval Architects.
M.R.S.H. .	Member Royal Society for Promotion of Health.
M.R.S.T. .	Member Royal Society of Teachers.
M.R.U.S.I. .	Member Royal United Service Institution.
M.S. .	Master of Surgery.
MS., MSS. .	Manuscript, Manuscripts.
M.S.C. .	Madras Staff Corps; Metropolitan Special Constabulary.
M.Sc. .	Master of Science.
M.S.D. .	Master Surgeon Dentist.
M.S.H. .	Master of Stag-Hounds.
M.S.M. .	Meritorious Service Medal.
M.T.B. .	Motor Torpedo-Boat.
M.T.P.I. .	Member Town Planning Institute.
Mus.B. .	Bachelor of Music.
Mus.D. .	Doctor of Music.
Mus.M. .	Master of Music.
M.V.O. .	Member Royal Victorian Order.
M.W.B. .	Metropolitan Water Board.
N.A. . .	National Academician (America).
N.A.A.F.I. .	Navy, Army and Air Force Institutes.
N.A.L.G.O. .	National and Local Government Officers' Association.
N.B.A. .	North British Academy.

N.C.B.	. .	National Coal Board.
N.C.U.	. .	National Cyclists' Union.
N.D.A.	. .	National Diploma in Agriculture.
N.E.C.Inst.	.	North-East Coast Institution of Engineers and Shipbuilders.
N.E.D.C.	. .	National Economic Development Council.
N.F.S.	. .	National Fire Service.
N.F.U.	. .	National Farmers' Union.
N.I.	. .	Northern Ireland; Native Infantry.
N.L.F.	. .	National Liberal Federation.
N.P.	. .	Notary Public.
N.R.A.	. .	National Rifle Association.
N.S.	. .	Nova Scotia; National Society.
N.S.A.	. .	National Skating Association.
N.S.C.	. .	National Savings Committee.
N.S.P.C.C.	.	National Society for Prevention of Cruelty to Children.
N.U.M.	. .	National Union of Mineworkers.
N.U.T.	. .	National Union of Teachers.
N.U.T.N.	. .	National Union of Trained Nurses.
N.U.W.W.	.	National Union of Women Workers.
N.Y.C.	. .	New York City.
O.B.E.	. .	Officer Order of the British Empire.
O.C.	. .	Officer Commanding.
O.C.T.U.	. .	Officer Cadet Training Unit.
O.E.D.	. .	Oxford English Dictionary.
O.F.M.	. .	Order of Friars Minor.
O.H.B.M.S.	.	On His (or Her) Britannic Majesty's Service.
O.H.M.S.	. .	On His (or Her) Majesty's Service.
O.L.	. .	Officer of the Order of Leopold.
O.M.	. .	Order of Merit.
O.M.I.	. .	Oblate of Mary Immaculate.
O.P.	. .	*Ordinis Prædicatorum* = of the Order of Preachers (Dominican ecclesiastical title).
O.S.A.	.	Ontario Society of Artists; Order of St. Augustine.
O.S.B.	. .	Order of St. Benedict.
O.S.D.	. .	Order of St. Dominic.
O.S.F.C.	. .	Order of St. Francis (Capuchin).
O.U.A.C.	. .	Oxford University Athletic Club.
O.U.A.F.C.	.	Oxford University Association Football Club.
O.U.B.C.	. .	Oxford University Boat Club.
O.U.C.C.	. .	Oxford University Cricket Club.
O.U.D.S.	. .	Oxford University Dramatic Society.
O.U.R.F.C.	.	Oxford University Rugby Football Club.

Oxon. . . . (Bishop of) Oxford; Oxfordshire.

P.C. . . . Privy Councillor.
P.C.M.O. . . Principal Colonial Medical Officer.
P.F. . . . Procurator-Fiscal.
Ph.B. . . . Bachelor of Philosophy.
Ph.C. . . . Pharmaceutical Chemist.
Ph.D. . . . Doctor of Philosophy.
P.M.G. . . Postmaster-General.
P.M.O. . . Principal Medical Officer.
P.M.R.A.F.N.S. . Princess Mary's Royal Air Force Nursing Service.
P.M.S.. . . President Miniature Society.
P.N.E.U. . . Parents' National Educational Union.
P.P.R.A. . . Past President of the Royal Academy.
P.P.S. . . . Parliamentary Private Secretary.
P.R.A.. . . President of the Royal Academy.
P.R.H.A. . . President Royal Hibernian Academy.
P.R.I. . . President Royal Institute of Painters in Water
                    Colours.
P.R.S. . . . President Royal Society.
P.R.S.A. . . President of the Royal Scottish Academy.
P.R.S.E. . . President Royal Society of Edinburgh.
Pte. . . . Private (soldier).
P.W.D. . . Public Works Department.

Q.A.L.A.S. . . Qualified Associate Chartered Land Agents' Society
Q.A.R.A.N.C. . Queen Alexandra's Royal Army Nursing Corps.
Q.A.R.N.N.S. . Queen Alexandra's Royal Naval Nursing Service.
Q.C. . . . Queen's Counsel.
Q.H.C. . . Honorary Chaplain to the Queen.
Q.H.P. . . Honorary Physician to the Queen.
Q.H.S. . . Honorary Surgeon to the Queen.
Q.M.G. . . Quartermaster-General.
Q.P.M. . . Queen's Police Medal.
Q.S. . . . Quarter Sessions; Queen's Scholar.

R.A. . . . Royal Academician; Royal Artillery.
R.A.A.F. . . Royal Australian Air Force.
R.A.C. . . Royal Armoured Corps; Royal Automobile Club;
                    Royal Agricultural College.
R.A.Ch.D. . . Royal Army Chaplains' Department.
R.A.D.C. . . Royal Army Dental Corps.
R.A.E.C. . . Royal Army Educational Corps.
R.A.F.. . . Royal Air Force.
R.A.F.R. . . Royal Air Force Regiment.

R.A.F.V.R.	.	.	Royal Air Force Volunteer Reserve.
R.A.M.	.	.	Royal Academy of Music.
R.A.M.C.	.	.	Royal Army Medical Corps.
R.A.N.	.	.	Royal Australian Navy.
R.A.O.C.	.	.	Royal Army Ordnance Corps.
R.A.P.C.	.	.	Royal Army Pay Corps.
R.A.S..	.	.	Royal Astronomical Society; Royal Asiatic Society.
R.Aux.A.F.	.	.	Royal Auxiliary Air Force.
R.A.V.C.	.	.	Royal Army Veterinary Corps.
R.B.	.	.	Rifle Brigade.
R.B.A..	.	.	Royal Society of British Artists.
R.B.C..	.	.	Royal British Colonial Society of Artists.
R.B.S..	.	.	Royal Society of British Sculptors.
R.C.	.	.	Roman Catholic.
R.C.A.F.	.	.	Royal Canadian Air Force.
R.Cam.A.	.	.	Member Royal Cambrian Academy.
R.C.M.P.	.	.	Royal Canadian Mounted Police.
R.C.N.	.	.	Royal Canadian Navy; Royal College of Nursing.
R.C.O.	.	.	Royal College of Organists.
R.C.P..	.	.	Royal College of Physicians.
R.C.S..	.	.	Royal College of Surgeons; Royal College of Science.
R.C.T..	.	.	Royal Corps of Transport.
R.C.V.S.	.	.	Royal College of Veterinary Surgeons.
R.D.	.	.	Rural Dean; Royal Naval Reserve Decoration.
R.D.C.	.	.	Rural District Council.
R.D.I..	.	.	Royal Designer for Industry.
R.E.	.	.	Royal Engineers; Fellow of Royal Society of Painter-Etchers and Engravers.
Reg.Prof.	.	.	Regius Professor.
R.E.M.E.	.	.	Royal Electrical and Mechanical Engineers.
R.F.A..	.	.	Royal Field Artillery.
R.G.A.	.	.	Royal Garrison Artillery.
R.G.S.	.	.	Royal Geographical Society.
R.H.A.	.	.	Royal Hibernian Academy; Royal Horse Artillery.
R.H.G.	.	.	Royal Horse Guards.
R.H.S.	.	.	Royal Humane Society; Royal Horticultural Society.
R.I.	.	.	Royal Institute of Painters in Water Colours; Rhode Island.
R.I.A..	.	.	Royal Irish Academy.
R.I.B.A.	.	.	Royal Institute of British Architects.
R.I.B.S.	.	.	Royal Institute of British Sculptors.
R.I.M..	.	.	Royal Indian Marine.
R.I.N..	.	.	Royal Indian Navy.
R.I.N.A.	.	.	Royal Institution of Naval Architects.

R.M.	.	Royal Marines; Resident Magistrate.
R.M.A.	.	Royal Marine Artillery; Royal Military Academy; Sandhurst (incorporating Royal Military Academy, Woolwich).
R.M.C.	.	Royal Military College, Sandhurst (now Royal Military Academy).
R.M.L.I.	.	Royal Marine Light Infantry.
R.M.S.	.	Royal Microscopical Society; Royal Mail Steamer, Royal Society of Miniature Painters.
R.M.S.M.	.	Royal Military School of Music.
R.N.	.	Royal Navy.
R.N.L.I.	.	Royal National Life-boat Institution.
R.N.R.	.	Royal Naval Reserve.
R.N.V.R.	.	Royal Naval Volunteer Reserve.
R.N.V.S.R.	.	Royal Naval Volunteer Supplementary Reserve.
R.N.Z.N.	.	Royal New Zealand Navy.
R.O.C.	.	Royal Observer Corps.
R.O.I.	.	Royal Institute of Oil Painters.
R.P.S.	.	Royal Photographic Society.
R.R.C.	.	Royal Red Cross (Lady of).
R.S.A.	.	Royal Scottish Academician; Royal Society of Arts.
R.S.E.	.	Royal Society of Edinburgh.
R.S.H.	.	Royal Society for Promotion of Health (formerly Royal Sanitary Institute).
R.S.L.	.	Royal Society of Literature.
R.S.M.	.	Regimental Sergeant-Major; Royal School of Mines; Royal Society of Medicine.
R.S.P.B.	.	Royal Society for Protection of Birds.
R.S.P.C.A.	.	Royal Society for the Prevention of Cruelty to Animals.
R.S.P.P.	.	Royal Society of Portrait Painters.
R.S.W.S.	.	Royal Scottish Water-Colour Society.
Rt. Hon.	.	Right Honourable.
R.T.O.	.	Railway Transport Officer.
Rt. Revd.	.	Right Reverend (of a Bishop).
R.T.R.	.	Royal Tank Regiment.
R.T.S.	.	Royal Toxophilite Society.
R.T.Y.C.	.	Royal Thames Yacht Club.
R.U.	.	Rugby Union.
R.U.I.	.	Royal University of Ireland.
R.U.R.	.	Royal Ulster Rifles.
R.U.S.I.	.	Royal United Service Institution.
R.V.C.	.	Royal Victorian Chain.
R.V.C.I.	.	Royal Veterinary College of Ireland.
R.W.A.	.	Member of Royal West of England Academy.
R.W.S.	.	Royal Society of Painters in Water Colours.

R.Y.S. .	.	Royal Yacht Squadron.
Sarum.	.	(Bishop of) Salisbury.
S.A.S.O.	.	Senior Air Staff Officer.
S.C.A.P.A.	.	Society for Checking the Abuses of Public Advertising.
Sc.B. .	.	Bachelor of Science.
Sc.D. .	.	Doctor of Science.
S.C.F. .	.	Senior Chaplain to the Forces.
S.C.L. .	.	Student in Civil Law.
S.C.M..	.	State Certified Midwife; Student Christian Movement.
S.D.F. .	.	Social Democratic Federation.
S.G. .	.	Solicitor-General; Scots Guards.
S.G.M.	.	Sea Gallantry Medal.
S.J. .	.	Society of Jesus (Jesuits).
S.L. .	.	Serjeant-at-Law.
S.M. .	.	Medal of Service (Canada).
S.M.E.	.	School of Military Engineering.
S.O. .	.	Staff Officer.
s.p. .	.	*Sine prole* (without issue).
S.P.C.K.	.	Society for Promoting Christian Knowledge.
S.P.G. .	.	Society for the Propagation of the Gospel (now U.S.P.G.).
S.P.Q.R.	.	*Senatus Populusque Romanus* (The Senate and People of Rome).
S.P.R. .	.	Society for Psychical Research.
S.P.R.C.	.	Society for Prevention and Relief of Cancer.
S.P.S.P.	.	St. Peter and St. Paul (The Papal Seal).
S.R. .	.	Special Reserve.
S.R.N.	.	State Registered Nurse.
S.R.O.	.	Supplementary Reserve of Officers.
S.R.S. .	.	Fellow of the Royal Society (*Societatis Regiæ Socius*).
S.S.C. .	.	Solicitor before Supreme Court (Scotland).
S.S.J.E.	.	Society of St. John the Evangelist.
S.S.M..	.	Society of the Sacred Mission.
S.S.U. .	.	Sunday School Union.
S.T.D..	.	*Sacræ Theologiæ Doctor* (Doctor of Sacred Theology); Subscriber Trunk Dialling.
S.T.L. .	.	*Sacræ Theologiæ Lector* (Reader or a Professor of Sacred Theology).
S.T.M.	.	*Sacræ Theologiæ Magister* (Master of Sacred Theology).
S.T.P. .	.	*Sacræ Theologiæ Professor* (Professor of Divinity, old form of D.D.).

T.A.	. .	Territorial Army.
T.A.A.	. .	Territorial Army Association.
T.&A.V.R.	. .	Territorial and Army Volunteer Reserve.
T.A.N.S.	. .	Territorial Army Nursing Service.
T.C.D.	. .	Trinity College, Dublin.
T.D.	. .	Territorial Decoration.
T.F.	. .	Territorial Forces.
T.I.H.	. .	Their Imperial Highnesses.
T.L.S.	. .	Territorial Long Service Medal.
T.R.C.	. .	Thames Rowing Club.
T.R.H.	. .	Their Royal Highnesses.
T.S.D.	. .	Tertiary of St. Dominick.
T.S.H.	. .	Their Serene Highnesses.
T.U.C.	. .	Trades Union Congress.
T.Y.C.	. .	Thames Yacht Club.

U.A.R.	. .	United Arab Republic.
U.C.	. .	University College.
U.D.C.	. .	Urban District Council.
U.F.	. .	United Free Church.
U.K.	. .	United Kingdom.
U.N.O.	. .	United Nations Organization.
U.N.E.S.C.O.	.	United Nations Educational, Scientific and Cultural Organization.
U.N.I.C.E.F.	.	United Nations International Children's Emergency Fund.
U.P.	. .	United Presbyterian.
U.P.C.	. .	United Presbyterian Church.
U.S.A.	. .	United States of America.
U.S.C.L.	. .	United Society for Christian Literature.
U.S.N.	. .	United States Navy.
U.S.P.G.	. .	United Society for the Propagation of the Gospel.
U.S.S.R.	. .	Union of Soviet Socialist Republics.

V.A.	. .	Victoria and Albert (The Royal Order of).
V.A.D.	. .	Voluntary Aid Detachment.
V.C.	. .	Victoria Cross.
V.D.	. .	Volunteer Officers' Decoration; Victorian Decoration; Royal Naval Volunteer Reserve Officers' Decoration (now V.R.D.).
Ven.	. .	Venerable (of an Archdeacon).
Very Revd.	. .	Very Reverend (of a Dean).
Vice-Adm.	. .	Vice-Admiral.
V.M.H.	. .	Victoria Medal of Honour (Royal Horticultural Society) for Horticulture.

V.P.	.	.	Vice-President.
V.R.	.	.	*Victoria Regina* (Queen Victoria).
V.R.D.	.	.	Royal Naval Volunteer Reserve Officers' Decoration.
V.R. et I.	.	.	*Victoria Regina et Imperatrix* (Victoria Queen and Empress).
W.A.A.C.	.	.	Women's Auxiliary Army Corps.
W.I.	.	.	West Indies; Women's Institute.
Winton.	.	.	(Bishop of) Winchester.
W.L.A.	.	.	Women's Land Army.
W.L.F.	.	.	Women's Liberal Federation.
W.O.	.	.	War Office.
W.R.A.C.	.	.	Women's Royal Army Corps.
W.R.A.F.	.	.	Women's Royal Air Force.
W.R.I.	.	.	Women's Rural Institute.
W.R.N.S.	.	.	Women's Royal Naval Service.
W.R.V.S.	.	.	Women's Royal Voluntary Service.
W.S.	.	.	Writer to the Signet.
W.S.P.U.	.	.	Women's Social and Political Union.
W.V.S.	.	.	Women's Voluntary Services (now W.R.V.S.)
Y.H.A.	.	.	Youth Hostels Association.
Y.M.C.A.	.	.	Young Men's Christian Association.
Y.W.C.A.	.	.	Young Women's Christian Association.

SOME PRONUNCIATIONS OF
PROPER NAMES

a	. .	as in cat
ah	. .	as in father
ay	. .	as in day
g	. .	as in good
i	. .	as in pin
ō	. .	as in home

o	. .	as in dog
ōō	. .	as in food
oo	. .	as in hood
ow	. .	as in how
y	. .	as in spy

Abergavenny	{ Aber-ga-*ven*-i (town). Aber-*gen*-i (title).
Abinger .	. *Ab*-binjer.
Acheson .	. *Ach*-ison.
Achonry .	. *Acon*-ri.
Ackroyd .	. *Ak*-roid.
Adye . .	. *Ay*-di.
Aflalo .	. Af-*lah*-lo.
Agate . .	. *Ay*-gat.
Ailesbury .	. *Ayls*-bri.
Ailsa . .	. *Ayl*-sa.
Aitchison .	. *Aych*-ison.
Akerman .	. *Ack*-erman.
Akers-Douglas .	. *Ay*-kers-*Dug*-glas.
Alcester .	. *Aw*-ster.
Aldenham .	. *Awl*-dnam.
Alington .	. *Al*-ington.
Alleyne .	. Al-*lane*, *Al*-len.
Allhusen .	. Al-*hew*-sen.
Alma-Tadema .	. *Al*-ma-*Tad*-dema.
Alnemouth .	. *Ayl*-mouth.
Alnwick .	. *An*-nick.
Alresford .	. *Awl*-sford.
Althorp .	. *Awl*-trup.
Altrincham .	. *Awl*-tringam.
Alveston .	. *Aw*-son.
Amory .	. *A*-mori.
Ampthill .	. *Amt*-hill.
Annaly .	. *An*-nali.
Annesley .	. *An*-sli.
Anstruther	{ *An*-ster, *An*-struther.
Antrobus .	. *An*-trobus.
Appuldurcombe	Appoldur-*cōōm*.
Arbuthnott .	. Ar-*buth*-not.

Archdall .	. *Arch*-dale.
Ardagh .	. *Ar*-da.
Ardee .	. Ar-*dee*.
Ardilaun .	. Ardi-*lawn*.
Argyll .	. Ar-*gyle*.
Armagh .	. Ar-*mah*.
Ashburnham .	. *Ash*-burnam.
Ashburton .	. *Ash*-burton.
Ashcombe .	. *Ash*-com.
Assheton .	. *Ash*-ton.
Athenry .	. Athen-*ry*.
Atherton .	. *Ath*-erton.
Athlumney .	. Ath-*lum*-ni.
Atholl .	. *Ath*-ol.
Avoch .	. Aukh.
Ayers .	. Airs.
Ayerst .	. *A*-urst.
Ayscough .	. *Ask*-ew.
Auchinleck	{ *Aff*-leck. *Awk*-inleck.
Auchterlonie .	. *Aukh*-ter-*lōn*-i.
Ava . .	. *Ah*-va.
Baden-Powell	. *Bay*-dn-*Pō*-ell.
Bagehot .	. *Baj*-jut.
Baggallay .	. *Bag*-gali.
Balcarres .	. Bal-*car*-riss.
Baldry .	. *Bawl*-dri.
Balfour .	. *Bal*-four.
Balgonie .	. Bal-*gō*-ni.
Balguy .	. *Bawl*-gi.
Balleny .	. Ba-*len*-i.
Bamfyld .	. *Bam*-feeld.
Barfreeston	. *Bar*-son.
Barham .	. *Bah*-ram.
Barnardiston .	. Barnar-*dis*-ton.

Barraclough	. *Bar*-racluff.
Barttelot .	. *Bart*-ilot.
Barugt .	. Barf.
Barwick .	. *Bar*-rick.
Bateson .	. *Bayt*-son.
Battye .	. *Bat*-ti.
Baugh .	. Baw.
Beaconsfield	*Beck*-onsfield (town). *Bee*-consfield (title).
Beatty .	. *Bee*-ti.
Beauchamp .	. *Bee*-cham.
Beauclerc .	. *Bō*-clare.
Beaufort .	. *Bō*-fort.
Beaulieu .	. *Bew*-li.
Beaumont .	. *Bō*-mont.
Beaworthy .	. *Bow*-ri.
Becke. .	. Beck.
Beckles .	. *Beck*-els.
Bedel .	. *Bee*-dle.
Belisha .	. Be-*lee*-sha.
Bellamy .	. *Bel*-lami.
Bellew .	*Bell*-yew. Bell-*oo*.
Bellingham .	. *Bell*-injam.
Belvoir .	. *Bee*-ver.
Berkeley .	. *Bark*-li.
Berkshire .	. *Bark*-shere.
Berners .	. *Ber*-ners.
Bertie. .	. *Bar*-ti.
Besant	*Bess*-ant. Be-*zant*.
Besley	*Beez*-li. *Bez*-li.
Bessborough .	. *Bez*-burra.
Bethune .	. *Bee*-ton.
Bicester .	. *Bis*-ter.
Biddulph .	. *Bid*-dulf.
Bigelow .	. *Big*-gelo.
Bispham .	. *Bis*-pam.
Blakiston .	. *Black*-iston.
Blois . .	. Bloyce.
Blomefield Blomfield	. *Bloom*-field.
Bloundelle .	. *Blun*-dell.
Blount .	. Blunt.
Blyth .	Bly. Blyth.
Blythborough	*Bly*-bra.
Bois . .	. Boyce.
Boisragon .	. *Bor*-ragon.
Boldre .	. *Bold*-er.
Boleyn	*Boo*-len. Bo-*linn*.
Bolingbroke	. *Bol*-linbrook.
Bolitho .	. Bo-*ly*-tho.
Bompas .	. *Bum*-pas.
Bonsor .	. *Bon*-sor.
Bonython .	. Bon-*y*-thon.
Boord .	. Bord.
Borrowes .	. *Bur*-rōs.
Borthwick.	. *Borth*-wick.
Bosanquet .	. *Bōzn*-ket.
Boscawen	Bo-*scō*-en. Bo-*scaw*-en.
Bosham .	. *Boz*-um.
Boughey .	. *Bow*-i.
Boughton .	*Bow*-ton. *Baw*-ton.
Boulger .	. *Bol*-jer.
Bourchier .	. *Bow*-cher.
Bourke .	. Berk.
Bourne .	Born. Bern. Bourn.
Bowles .	. Boles.
Brabazon .	. *Brab*-bazon.
Brabourne.	. *Bray*-bn.
Brahan .	. Brawn.
Breadalbane	. Bred-*awl*-ban.
Brechin .	. *Breek* hin.
Broke .	. Brook.
Brough .	. Bruff.
Brougham.	. Broom.
Broughton	. *Braw*-ton.
Buccleuch .	. Bu-*cloo*.
Buchan .	. *Buk*-han.
Buchanan .	. Bu-*can*-non.

Burbury	.	*Ber*-bery.
Burges	.	*Ber*-jez.
Burghclere		*Ber*-clair.
Burghersh		*Ber*-gersh.
Burghley	.	*Ber*-li.
Burroughes		*Bur*-roze.
Burtchaell		*Ber*-chell.
Bury .	.	{*Ber*-ri. *Bew*-ri.
Buszard	.	*Buz*-zard.
Bythesea	.	*Bith*-see.
Cadogan	.	Ka-*dug*-gan.
Cahill	.	*Kay*-hill.
Caillard	.	*Ky*-ar.
Caius .	.	Kees.
Caldcleugh		*Kahld*-cluff.
Calderon	.	*Kawld*-eron.
Calthorpe	.	*Kawl*-thorp.
Camoys	.	Kam-*oys*.
Campden	.	*Kam*-den.
Capell	.	*Kay*-pel.
Carbery	.	*Kar*-beri.
Carew	.	{*Kair*-i. Kar-*oo*.
Carlyon	.	Kar-*ly*-on.
Carmichael		Kar-*my*-kal.
Carnegie	.	Kar-*neg*-gi.
Carnwath	.	*Karn*-woth.
Carpmael	.	*Karp*-male.
Carruthers	.	Kar-*ruth*-ers.
Carshalton		Kay-*shaw*-ton.
Carysfort	.	*Kar*-risfort.
Cassilis	.	*Kas*-sels.
Castlereagh	.	*Kah*-selray.
Cavan	.	*Kav*-van.
Cavanagh	.	*Kav*-vana.
Chalmers	.	*Chah*-mers.
Chaloner	.	*Chal*-loner.
Chandos	.	*Shan*-dos.
Charlemont		*Charl*-mont.
Charteris	.	{*Char*-teris. *Char*-ters.
Chaworth	.	*Chah*-worth.
Cheetham	.	*Cheet*-am.
Chenies	.	*Chay*-niz.
Cherwell	.	*Char*-well.
Chetwode	.	*Chet*-wood.
Chetwynd	.	*Chet*-wind.
Cheylesmore		*Chil*-smor.
Cheyne	.	*Chay*-ni.
Chichele	.	*Chich*-eli.
Chiene	.	Sheen.
Chirrol	.	*Chir*-rol.
Chisholm	.	*Chiz*-zom.
Chiswick	.	*Chiz*-ik.
Cholmeley Cholmondeley Chomley	}	*Chum*-li.
Cirencester		{*Syr*-ensester. *Siss*-iter. *Sis*-sister.
Clanricarde	.	Klan-*rick*-ard.
Clarina	.	Kla-*reen*-a.
Claverhouse	.	*Klay*-vers.
Clerk .	.	Klark.
Clerke	.	Klark.
Clery .	.	*Klee*-ri.
Cliveden	.	*Kliv*-den.
Clogher	.	Klo-her.
Clonbrock	.	Klon-*brock*.
Cloncurry	.	Klun-*cur*-ri.
Clonmell	.	Klon-*mel*.
Clough	.	Kluff.
Clowes		{Klews. Klows.
Clwyd	.	*Klew*-id.
Cochrane	.	*Kock*-ran.
Cockburn	.	*Ko*-burn.
Cogenhoe	.	*Kook*-no.
Coghill	.	*Kog*-hill.
Coke .	.	{Kook. Koke.
Colborne	.	*Kole*-burn.
Colclough	.	*Koke*-li.
Colles	.	*Kol*-lis.
Colnaghi	.	Kol-*nah*-gi.
Colquhoun	.	Ko-*hoon*.
Colville	.	*Koll*-vil.

Combe	. Koom.
Compton	. *Kump*-ton.
Congresbury	. *Koom*-sbri.
Conisborough	. *Kun*-sbra.
Constable	. *Kun*-stable.
Conyngham	. *Kun*-ningam.
Copleston	. *Kop*-pelston.
Corcoran	. *Kork*-ran.
Cottenham	. *Kot*-tenam.
Cottesloe	. *Kot*-slo.
Couch	. Kooch.
Courtenay⎱ Courtney ⎰	. *Kort*-ni.
Courthope	. *Kort*-ope.
Courtown	. *Kor*-town.
Cousens	. *Kuz*-zens.
Coutts	. Kōōts.
Coventry	⎰*Kov*-entri. ⎱*Kuv*-entri.
Coverdale	. *Kuv*-erdale.
Coverley	. *Kuv*-erli.
Cowell	⎰*Kow*-ell. ⎱*Kō*-ell.
Cowen	⎰*Kō*-en. ⎱*Kow*-en.
Cowles	. Koles.
Cowper	⎰*Kōō*-per. ⎱*Kow*-per.
Cozens	. *Kuz*-zens.
Crawshay	. *Kraw*-shay.
Creagh	. Kray.
Creighton	. *Kry*-ton.
Crespigny	. *Krep*-ni.
Crichton	. *Kry*-ton.
Croghan	. *Krō*-an.
Cromartie	. *Krum*-marti.
Crombie	. *Krum*-bi.
Culme-Seymour	*Kulm*-*See*-mer.
Cuningham ⎱ Cuninghame ⎬ Cunyngham ⎰	. *Kun*-ningam.
Curteis ⎱ Curtois ⎰	. *Ker*-tis.
Czaplicka	. Chap-*lit*-ska.

Dacre	. *Day*-ker.
Dacres	. *Day*-kers.
D'Aguilar	. *Dag*-willer.
Dalbiac	. *Dawl*-biac.
Dalgleish	. Dal-*gleesh*.
Dalhousie	. Dal-*how*-zi.
Dalmeny	. Dal-*men*-ni.
Dalrymple	. Dal-*rim*-ple.
Dalziel	⎰Dee-*ell*. ⎱Dal-*zeel*.
Daubeney	. *Daw*-bni.
Daventry	. *Dain*-tri.
Dealtry	. *Dawl*-tri.
Dease	. Dees.
Death	. De-*ath*.
De Bathe	. De Bahth.
De Blaquiere	. De *Black*-yer.
De Burgh	. De Berg.
Decies	. *Dee*-shees.
De Crespigny	. De *Krep*-ni.
De La Pasture	. De *Lap*-pature.
De la Poer	. De la Poor.
De la Warr	. *De*-lawar.
De l'Isle	. De Lyle.
De Mauley	. De *Maw*-li.
De Moleyns	. *Dem*-moleens.
De Montalt	. Demon-*talt*.
De Montmorency	De Muntmor-*en*-si.
Denbigh	. *Den*-bi.
Dennehy	. *Den*-nehee.
Derby	. *Dar*-bi.
Dering	. *Deer*-ing.
De Rohan	. De *Ro*-an.
De Ros	. De Roos.
Derwent	. *Dar*-went.
De Salis	⎰De *Sal*-lis. ⎱De Sahls.
Desart	. *Des*-sart.
De Saumarez ⎱ De Sausmarez ⎰	De *So*-marez.
Des Voeux	. Day-*vō*.
Devereux	⎰*Dev*-veroo. ⎱*Dev*-veroox.
De Vesci	. De *Vess*-i.

D'Eyncourt	.	*Dain*-curt.	Egerton .	. *Ej*-erton.
De Zoete .	.	De Zōōt.	Elam . .	. *Ee*-lam.
Dicksee .	.	*Dick*-si.	Elcho. .	. *El*-ko.
Dillwyn .	.	*Dil*-lon.	Elibank .	. *El*-libank.
Diosy .	.	De-ō-zi.	Eliot . .	. *Eli*-iot.
Disraeli .	.	Diz-*rail*-i.	Ellesmere .	. *Els*-meer.
Domvile .	.	*Dum*-vill.	Elphinstone	. *El*-finston.
Donegal .	.	*Don*-igawl.	Enniskillen	. In-nis-*kil*-len.
Doneraile .	.	*Dun*-erayl.	Ernle .	. *Ern*-li.
Donoghue .	.	*Dun*-nohoo.	Esmonde .	. *Ez*-mond.
Donoughmore	.	*Dun*-nomor.	Etheredge .	. *Eth*-erij.
Doudney .	.	*Dewd*-ni.	Evershed .	. *Ev*-ershed.
Dougall .	.	*Doo*-gal.	Ewart .	. *U*-art.
Doughty .	.	*Dow*-ti.	Eyam .	. Eem.
Douglas .	.	*Dug*-las.	Eyre .	. Air.
Dowie .	.	*Dow*-i.	Eyton .	. *Y*-ton.
Drogheda .	.	*Draw*-eda.		
Du Buisson	.	*Dew*-bisson.	Faed . .	. Fade.
Du Cane .	.	Dew *Kane*.	Falconbridge	. *Fawk*-onbrij.
Duchesne .	.	Du-*kahn*.	Falconer .	. *Fawk*-ner.
Ducie. .	.	*Dew*-ssi.	Falkland .	. *Fawk*-land.
Dumaresq	.	Doo-*mer*-rick.	Farquhar .	{*Fark*-wer.
Dumfries .	.	Dum-*freess*.		{*Fark*-er.
Dunalley .	.	Dun-*nal*-li.	Farquharson	{*Fark*-werson.
Dundas .	.	Dun-*das*.		{*Fark*-erson.
Dungarvan	.	Dun-*gar*-van.	Fawcett .	{*Faw*-set.
Dunglass .	.	Dun-*glass*.		{*Foss*-et.
Dunmore .	.	Dun-*mor*.	Fearon .	. *Fear*-on.
Dunsany .	.	Dun-*sa*-ni.	Featherston-	*Feth*-erstonhaw,
Duntze .	.	Dunts.	haugh	sometimes *Fan*-
Du Plat .	.	Dew *Plah*.		shaw.
Dupplin .	.	*Dup*-plin.	Feilden .	. *Feel*-den.
Du Quesne	.	Dew *Kane*.	Feilding .	. *Feel*-ding.
Durand .	.	Dew-*rand*.	Fenwick .	. *Fen*-ick.
Durrant .	.	Dur-*rant*.	Fermanagh	. *Fer*-mana.
Dymoke .	.	*Dim*-muk.	Feversham .	. *Fav*-ersham.
Dynevor .	.	*Din*-nevor.	Ffolkes .	. Fokes.
Dysart .	.	*Dy*-sart.	Ffoulkes .	{Fokes.
				{Fōōks.
Eames .	.	Eems.	Ffrangcon.	. *Frank*-on.
Eardley-Wilmot	*Erd*-li-*Wil*-mot.	Fiennes .	. Fynes.
Ebrington .		*Ebb*-rington.	Fildes .	. Fylds.
Ebury .	.	*Ee*-beri.	Findlater .	. *Fin*-litter.
Edgcumbe	.	*Ej*-cum.	Findlay .	. *Fin*-li.
Edridge .	.	*Edd*-rij.	Fingall .	. *Fin*-gawl.

Fitzhardinge	. Fitz-*hard*-ing.	Giffard	.	{*Gif*-fard. / *Jif*-fard.
Fitzwygram	. Fitz-*wy*-gram.			
Fleming	. *Flem*-ming.	Gildea	.	{*Gil*-di. / Gil-*day*.
Fludyer	. *Flud*-yer.			
Foljambe	. *Fool*-jam.	Gilhooly	. Gil-*hoo*-li.
Forbes	. Forbs.	Gilkes	. Jilks.
Fortescue	. *Fort*-iskew.	Gill	. .	{Gill. / Jill.
Foulis	. Fowls.			
Fowey	. Foy.	Gilles	. *Gill*-is.
Fowke	. Foke.	Gillespie	. Gill-*ess*-pi.
Francillon	. Fran-*sil*-lon.	Gillingham	. *Jill*-ingam.
Freake	. Freek.	Gilmour	. *Gil*-mor.
Freke	. Freck.	Gilroy	. *Gil*-roy.
Fremantle	. Free-*man*-tle.	Gilzean	. Gil-*een*.
Freyer	{*Free*-ar. / *Fry*-er.	Glamis	. Glahms.
		Glanely	. Glan-*el*-i.
Froude	. Frŏŏd.	Glenmuick	. Glen-*mick*.
Furneaux	. *Fur*-no.	Glenquoich	. Glen-*ko*-i.
		Glerawly	. Gler-*aw*-li.
Gairdner	. *Gard*-ner.	Gloag	. Glōg.
Galbraith	. Gal-*brayth*.	Goldsworthy	. *Gōls*-worthi.
Gallagher	. *Gal*-laher.	Gomme	. Gom.
Gallwey / Galway	. *Gawl*-way.	Gorges	. *Gor*-jiz.
		Gormanston	. *Gor*-manston.
Garioch	. *Ger*-ri.	Goschen	. *Gō*-shen.
Garmoyle	. Gar-*moyl*.	Goudy	. *Gow*-di.
Garnock	. *Gar*-nock.	Gough	. Goff.
Garvagh	. *Gar*-va.	Goulburn	. *Gōōl*-burn.
Garvice	. *Gar*-vis.	Gourley	. *Goor*-li.
Gatacre	. *Gat*-taker.	Gower	. Gaw, also as spelt.
Gathorne	. *Gay*-thorn.	Graeme	. Grame.
Geddes	. *Ged*-diz.	Graham / Grahame	. *Gray*-am.
Gee	. .	{Gee. / Jee.		
		Granard	. *Gran*-nard.
Geikie	. *Gee*-ki.	Greaves	. Graves.
Gell	. .	{Gell. / Jell.	Greenhalgh	. *Green*-how.
		Greig	. Greg.
Geoghegan	. *Gay*-gun.	Gresley	. *Gres*-li.
Gerard	. *Jer*-rard.	Greville	. *Grev*-el.
Gervis-Meyrick	*Jer*-vis-*Mer*-rick.	Grier	. Greer.
Gethen / Gethin / Gething	{*Geth*-in. / *Geeth*-in.	Grosvenor	. *Grove*-nor.
		Guildford	. *Gil*-ford.
		Guillamore	. *Gill*-amor.
Gibbes	. Gibbs.	Guillemard	. *Gil*-mar.
Giddens	. *Gid*-dens.	Guinness	. *Gin*-iss.

Gwatkin	.	*Gwot*-kin.
Gye .	.	Jy.
Haden	.	*Hay*-dn.
Haggard	.	*Hag*-gard.
Haigh	.	Hayg.
Haldane	.	*Hawl*-dane.
Haldon	.	*Hawl*-don.
Halkett	.	*Hack*-et.
Hallé .	.	*Hal*-lay.
Halsbury	.	*Hawl*-sbri.
Halsey		⎰*Hawl*-si. ⎱*Hal*-si.
Hambro	.	*Ham*-boro.
Hamond	.	*Ham*-mond.
Hampden	.	*Ham*-den.
Hanbury	.	*Han*-buri.
Harberton	.	*Har*-berton.
Harcourt	.	*Har*-curt.
Hardinge	.	*Har*-ding.
Hardres	.	Hards.
Harenc	.	Har-*on*.
Harewood	.	*Har*-wood.
Harington	.	*Ha*-rington.
Harlech	.	*Har*-li.
Hawarden		⎰*Hay*-warden. ⎱*Har*-den.
Haweis		⎰*Haw*-is. ⎱Hoys.
Hayhurst	.	Hurst.
Hazlerigg	.	*Hay*-zelrig.
Headlam	.	*Hed*-lam.
Heathcote	.	*Heth*-cot.
Heberden	.	*Heb*-erden.
Hegarty	.	*Heg*-arti.
Heneage	.	*Hen*-ij.
Hennessey Hennessy		. *Hen*-essi.
Henniker	.	*Hen*-iker.
Henriques	.	Hen-*reek*-iz.
Hepburn	.	*Heb*-burn.
Herkomer	.	*Herk*-omer.
Herlihig	.	*Herl*-a-hee.
Herries	.	*Her*-ris.
Herschell	.	*Her*-shel.
Hertford	.	*Har*-ford.

Hervey	.	⎰*Her*-vi. ⎱*Har*-vi.
Heytesbury	.	*Hayt*-sburi.
Hills-Johnes	.	*Hills*-Jones.
Hindlip	.	*Hind*-lip.
Hobart		⎰*Hō*-bart. ⎱*Hub*-bart.
Hoey .	.	Hoy.
Hogan	.	*Ho*-gan.
Holbech	.	*Hol*-beech.
Holmes	.	Homes.
Holmesdale	.	*Home*-sdale.
Holm-Patrick	.	Home-Patrick.
Home	.	Hume.
Honyman	.	*Hun*-niman.
Honywood	.	*Hun*-niwood.
Hopetoun	.	*Hope*-ton.
Hotham	.	*Huth*-am.
Hough	.	Huff.
Houghton		⎰Huf-ton. ⎪*Haw*-ton. ⎨*How*-ton. ⎱*Ho*-ton.
Houston	.	*Hoost*-on.
Howorth	.	*How*-erth.
Hugessen	.	*Hew*-jessen.
Huish	.	*Hew*-ish.
Humphrey	.	*Hum*-fri.
Hunstanton	.	*Hun*-ston.
Huth .	.	*Hōōth*.
Hyndman	.	*Hynd*-man.
Iddesleigh	.	*Id*-sli.
Ightham	.	*Y*-tam.
Inchiquin	.	*Inch*-quin.
Inge .	.	Ing.
Ingelow	.	*In*-jelow.
Ingestre	.	*In*-gestri.
Ingham	.	*Ing*-am.
Inglis	.	*In*-gools.
Innes .	.	*In*-nis.
Inveraray	.	Inver-*air*-i.
Inverarity	.	Inver-*arr*-iti.
Isitt .	.	*Y*-sit.
Iveagh	.	*Y*-va.
Jacoby	.	*Jack*-obi.

Jeaffreson .	.	*Jeff*-erson.
Jeffreys	.	*Jef*-riz.
Jekyll.	.	*Jee*-kel.
Jerome	.	Jer-*ome*.
Jervaulx	.	*Jer*-vis.
Jervis.	.	*Jar*-vis.
Jervois	.	*Jar*-vis.
Jeune	.	Joon.
Jeyes .	.	Jays.
Jocelyn	.	*Joss*-lin.
Jolliffe	.	*Joll*-if.
Julyan	.	*Jōō*-lian.
Juta .	.	*Jōō*-ta.

Keatinge .	.	*Keet*-ing.
Keighley .	.	*Keeth*-li.
Keightley .	.	*Keet*-li.
Keiller	.	*Kee*-ler.
Kekewich .	.	*Keck*-wich.
Kennard	.	Ken-*ard*.
Kenyon	.	*Ken*-ion.
Keogh	.	K-*yeo*.
Keough⎫		
K'Eogh ⎬ .		*Kee*-ō.
Kehoe ⎭		
Keig .	.	Keeg.
Kernahan .	.	*Kern*-ahan.
Kesteven .	.	*Kest*-even.
Keynes	.	Kayns.
Kilchurn .	.	Kil-*ho*-orn.
Killanin .	.	Kill-*an*-in.
Kilmorey .	.	Kil-*mur*-ri.
Kincairney .	.	Kin-*cair*-ni.
Kingscote .	.	*Kings*-cut.
Kinnaird .	.	Kin-*naird*.
Kinnear .	.	Kin-*near*.
Kinnoull .	.	Kin-*nool*.
Kirkcudbright .	.	Kirk-*oo*-bri.
Kneen	.	Neen.
Knightly .	.	*Nyt*-ly.
Knighton .	.	*Ny*-ton.
Knockdow .	.	Nok-*doo*.
Knollys⎫		
Knowles⎭	.	Noles.
Knutsford .	.	*Nuts*-ford.

Knyvett	.	*Niv*-vet.
Kortright .	.	*Kort*-rite.
Kough	.	*Kee*-ō.
Kylsant	.	*Kil*-sant.
Kynaston .	.	*Kin*-naston.
Kynsey	.	*Kin*-si.

Labalmondiere		La-*bal*-mondeer.
Lacon	.	*Lay*-kon.
Laffan	.	La-*ffan*.
Lamington .	.	*Lay*-mington.
Langrishe .	.	*Lang*-rish.
Larpent	.	*Lar*-pent.
Lascelles .	.	*Las*-sels.
Lathom	.	*Lay*-thom.
Laughton .	.	*Law*-ton.
Lavengro .	.	*Lav*-engro.
Lawrence .	.	*Lor*-rence.
Layard	.	Laird.
Lea .	.	Lee.
Learmonth .	.	*Ler*-munth.
Leatham .	.	*Leeth*-am.
Leathes	.	⎰Leeths.
		⎱*Leeth*-iz.
Lebus	.	*Lee*-bus.
Lechmere .	.	*Leech*-meer.
Leconfield .	.	*Lek*-onfield.
Le Fanu	.	*Leff*-noo.
Lefevre	.	Le-*fee*-ver.
Lefroy	.	Le-*froy*.
Legard	.	*Lej*-ard.
Legge	.	Leg.
Legh .	.	Lee.
Lehmann .	.	*Lay*-man.
Leicester .	.	*Lest*-er.
Leigh	.	Lee.
Leighton .	.	*Lay*-ton.
Leinster .	.	⎰*Len*-ster.
		⎱*Lin*-ster.
Leishman .	.	*Leesh*-man.
Leiston	.	*Lay*-son.
Leitrim .	.	*Leet*-rim.
Leland	.	*Lee*-land.
Lemesurier .	.	Le-*mézurer*.
Leominster .	.	*Lem*-ster.
Le Patourel .	.	Le-*pat*-turel.

Le Poer	.	Le-*por*.
Le Queux	.	Le *Kew*.
Leven	.	*Lee*-ven.
Leverhulme	.	*Lee*-verhewm.
Leveson-Gower		*Lōō*-son-Gaw.
Levey	.	{*Lee*-vi. *Lev*-vi.
Ley	.	. Lee.
Leyland	.	*Lay*-land.
Lingen	.	*Ling*-en.
Lisle	.	{Lyle. Leel.
Listowel	.	*Lis*-tol.
Llangattock	.	Klan-*gat*-tock.
Llewellyn	.	Loo-*ell*-in.
Lochiel	.	Lok-*heel*.
Lochinbar	.	Lok-*hin*-bar.
Logue	.	*Lōg*.
Lough	.	Luff.
Loughborough		*Luf*-burra.
Lovat	.	*Luv*-at.
Lovibond	.	*Luv*-band.
Lowis	.	*Lōw*-is.
Lowther	.	*Lō*-ther.
Lugard	.	Loo-*gard*.
Lutwyche	.	*Lut*-wich.
Lydekker	.	Li-*deck*-er.
Lygon	.	*Lig*-gon.
Lymington	.	*Lim*-mington.
Lympne	.	Lim.
Lynam	.	*Ly*-nam.
Lysaght	.	*Ly*-sat or *Ly*-sacht.
Lysons	.	*Ly*-sons.
Lyveden	.	*Liv*-den.
Macalister	.	Mac-*al*-ister.
Macara	.	Mac-*ah*-ra.
McCorquodale	.	Ma-*cork*-odale.
Maccullagh	.	Ma-*cul*-la.
Macdona	.	Mac-*dun*-na.
M'Culloch	.	Ma-*cul*-lokh.
M'Eachern	.	Mac-*kek*-run.
McEvoy	.	*Mack*-evoy.
M'Ewan M'Ewen		Mac-*kew*-an.

M'Gee M'Ghee	.	Ma-*gee*.
MacGillivray	.	Ma-*gil*-veri.
M'Gillycuddy	.	*Mack*-licuddi.
Machell	.	*May*-chell.
Machen	.	*May*-chen.
M'Ilwraith	.	*Mack*-ilrayth.
MacIver M'Ivor	.	Mack-y-ver.
Mackarness	.	*Mack*-aness.
McKay	.	Mac-*ky*.
Mackie	.	*Mack*-i.
Maclachlan	.	Mac-*laukh*-lan.
Maclagan	.	Mac-*lag*-gan.
Maclaren	.	Mac-*lar*-ren.
Maclean	.	Ma-*clayn*.
Maclear	.	Ma-*cleer*.
Macleay	.	Ma-*clay*.
Macleod	.	Ma-*clowd*.
Macmahon	.	Mac-*mahn* (with internal h).
Macnamara	.	Macna-*mah*-ra.
M'Naught	.	Mac-*nawt*.
MacNaughton	.	Mac-*naw*-ton.
Macneill	.	Mac-*neel*.
Maconchy	.	Ma-*conk*-i.
Maconochie	.	Mack-*on*-okhi.
Macrorie	.	Mac-*rori*.
Madan	.	*Mad*-dan.
Maeterlinck	.	*Mah*-terlink.
Magdalen	.	*Mawd*-lin.
Magheramorne	.	*Mar*-ramorn.
Magnac	.	*Man*-niac.
Magrath	.	Ma-*grah*.
Maguire	.	Ma-*gwire*.
Mahan	.	Mahn.
Mahon	.	Ma-*hoon*.
Mahony	.	*Mah*-ni.
Mainwaring	.	*Man*-nering.
Majendie	.	*Maj*-endi.
Malet	.	*Mal*-let.
Mall, The	.	Mal, The.
Malmesbury	.	*Mahm*-sbri.
Manora	.	Man-*ur*-a.
Mansergh	.	*Man*-zer.

Marindin .	.	*Mar*-indin.
Marischal .	.	*Marsh*-al.
Marjoribanks	.	*March*-banks.
Marlborough	.	*Mawl*-bra.
Martineau .	.	*Mart*-ino.
Masham .	.	*Mash*-am.
Maskelyne.	.	*Mask*-elin.
Mather .	.	*May*-ther.
Matheson .	.	*Math*-ison. / *Mat*-tison.
Maturin .	.	*Mat*-turin.
Maugham .	.	Mawm.
Maughan .	.	Mawn.
Maunsell .	.	*Man*-sell.
Maurice .	.	*Mor*-ris.
Mayo .	.	*May*-o.
Meagher .	.	Maker.
Meath .	.	Meeth.
Meiklejohn	.	*Mick*-eljon.
Meldrum .	.	*Mel*-drum.
Melhuish .	.	*Mel*-lish.
Menpes .	.	*Men*-piz.
Menzies .	.	*Meng*-iz. / *Menz*-iz. / *Ming*-iz.
Meopham .	.	*Mep*-pam.
Mereworth	.	*Merri*-worth.
Methwold .	.	*Mew*-al.
Meurant .	.	Mew-*rant*.
Meux .	.	Mewz.
Meyer .	.	*My*-er.
Meynell .	.	*Men*-nel.
Meyrick .	.	*Mer*-rick.
Meysey- Thompson		*May*-zi- *Toms*-on.
Michelham .	.	*Mich*-lam.
Michie .	.	*Mik*-ki.
Mildmay .	.	*Myld*-may.
Millard .	.	Mil-*lard*.
Milles .	.	Mills.
Milngavie .	.	Mull-*gy*.
Mivart .	.	*My*-vart.
Molyneux .	.	*Mol*-neux. / *Mol*-new.
Momerie .	.	*Mum*-meri.
Monaghan .	.	*Mon*-nahan.
Monck .	.	Munk.
Monckton .	.	*Munk*-ton.
Moncrieff .	.	Mon-*creef*.
Monkhouse .	.	*Munk*-hows.
Monkswell .	.	*Munk*-swell.
Monro / Monroe	.	Mun-*ro*.
Monson .	.	*Mun*-son.
Montagu .	.	*Mont*-agew. / *Munt*-agew.
Monteagle.	.	Mun-*tee*-gle.
Montefiore	.	Montifi-*or*-i.
Montgomery	.	Munt-*gum*-meri.
Montresor.	.	Mont-*rez*-or.
Monzie .	.	Mun-*ee*.
Moran .	.	*Mor*-an.
Morant .	.	Mo-*rant*.
Moray .	.	*Mur*-ri.
Mordaunt .	.	*Mor*-dunt.
Morice .	.	*Mor*-ris.
Morrell .	.	Murr-*ell*.
Mostyn .	.	*Moss*-tin.
Mouat .	.	*Moo*-at.
Moule .	.	Mole.
Moulton .	.	*Mōl*-ton.
Mountmorres .	.	Mount-*mor*-ris.
Mowat .	.	*Mo*-at. / *Moo*-at.
Mowbray .	.	*Mow*-bri. / *Moo*-bri.
Moynihan .	.	*Moy*-ni-han.
Muncaster .	.	*Mun*-kaster.
Murfree .	.	*Mer*-fri.
Naas . .	.	Nace.
Naesmyth .	.	*Nay*-smith.
Naper .	.	*Nap*-per.
Napier .	.	*Nay*-pier. / Na-*peer*.
Neave .	.	Neev.
Neil . .	.	Neel.
Nepean .	.	Ne-*peen*.
Newburgh .	.	*New*-bra.
Newnes .	.	Newns.
Nias . .	.	*Nee*-as.

Nigel	.	*Ny*-jel.
Niven	.	*Niv*-ven.
Northbourne	.	*North*-burn.
Northcote	.	*North*-cot.
Nunburnholme		Nun-*bern*-um.

O'Callaghan	.	*Ocall*-ahan.
Ochterlony	.	Octerl-*o*-ni.
O'Dea	.	O'-*Day*.
O'Donoghue	.	O-*dun*-nahoo.
Ogilvy	.	O-gelvi.
O'Hagan	.	O-*hay*-gan.
Olivier	.	O-*liv*-vier.
O'Meara	.	O-*mah*-ra.
O'Morchoe	.	O-*mur*-roo.
Onions	.	{O-*ny*-ons. / *Un*-ions.
Ormelie	.	*Orm*-eli.
Ormonde	.	*Or*-mond.
Osbourne	.	*Os*-burn.
O'Shaughnessy		{O-*shaw*-nessi. / O-*shawk*-nessi.
Ouless	.	*Oo*-less.
Outram	.	*Oo*tram.

Paget	. .	*Paj*-it.
Pakenham	.	*Pack*-enum.
Palairet	.	*Pal*-laret.
Palgrave	.	Pal-grave.
Palles	.	*Pal*-liz.
Parnell	.	*Par*-nal.
Pasley	.	*Pay*-zli.
Paterson	.	*Pat*-terson.
Paton	.	*Pay*-ton.
Pauncefote	.	*Powns*-foot.
Pease	. .	Peez.
Pechell	.	*Pee*-chel.
Pegram	.	*Pee*-gram.
Pembroke	.	*Pem*-brook.
Pennefather	.	*Pen*-nifether.
Pennycuick		{*Pen*-nicook. / *Pen*-niquick.
Penrhyn	.	Pen-*rin*.
Pepys	.	{Peeps (ancient). / *Pep*-piss (modern)
Pery	. .	*Peer*-i.

Peto	. .	*Pee*-tō.
Petre	. .	*Pee*-ter.
Petrie	. .	*Pee*-tri.
Phayre	.	Fair.
Pierpoint	.	Peerpont.
Pierrepoint		Peerpont.
Pigou	. .	Pi-*goo*.
Pinero	.	Pin-*eer*-o.
Pipon	. .	*Pee*-pong.
Pirbright	.	*Per*-brite.
Pirie	. .	Pirri.
Pleydell-Bouverie		} *Pled*-el *Boo*-veri.
Pochin	.	*Putch*-in.
Pole	. .	Pool.
Pole Carew		Pool *Cair*-i.
Poltimore	.	*Pol*-timor.
Polwarth	.	*Pole*-werth.
Ponsonby	.	*Pun*-sunbi.
Pontefract	.	*Pum*-fret.
Poolewe	.	*Pool*-yoo.
Portal	.	*Por*-tal.
Porteous	.	*Por*-tius.
Portishead	.	*Poz*-zet.
Poulett	.	*Pau*-let.
Powell	.	*Po*-ell.
Powerscourt		*Poor*-scort.
Powlett	.	*Paw*-let.
Powys	.	*Po*-is.
Praed	.	Prade.
Pretyman	.	*Prut*-timan.
Prevost	.	*Prev*-vo.
Prideaux	.	{*Pree*-do. / *Prid*-dux. / *Prid*-do.
Probyn	.	*Pro*-bin.
Prothero	.	*Proth*-ero.
Provand	.	*Pro*-vand.
Prowse	.	Prowz.
Pugh	. .	Pew.
Puleston	.	*Pil*-ston.
Pulleine	.	*Pool*-len.
Pulteney	.	*Pult*-ni.
Pwllheli	.	*Pool*-thelli.
Pytchley	.	*Pych*-li.

Ralegh	.	*Raw*-li. / *Ral*-li.
Ralph.	.	Ralf. / Rafe.
Ranelagh	. .	*Ran*-ela.
Ranfurly	. .	*Ran*-ferli.
Ranjitsinhji		*Ran*-jit-*sin*-ji.
Rashleigh	. .	*Rash*-li.
Rathdonnell		Rath-*don*-nel.
Rathmore	.	Rath-*mor*.
Rayleigh	. .	*Ray*-li.
Raynham	. .	*Rain*-am.
Reading	. .	*Red*-ing.
Reay	. . .	Ray.
Rehan	. .	*Ree*-han.
Reichel	. .	*Ryk*-hel.
Renwick	. .	*Ren*-nick.
Reuter	. .	*Roy*-ter.
Rhind	. .	Rynd.
Rhondda	. .	*Ron*-tha.
Rhys	. .	Rees. / Rice.
Riach	. .	*Ree*-ack.
Riddell	. .	*Rid*-dle.
Ridehalgh	.	*Rid*-ō.
Rievaulx	. .	*Riv*-els.
Robartes	. .	Ro-*barts*.
Roche	. .	Roche.
Rodon	. .	*Rō*-don.
Rolleston	.	*Rol*-ston.
Romilly	. .	*Rom*-ili.
Romney	. .	*Rum*-ni. / *Rom*-ni.
Ronaldshay	.	Ron-*ald*-shay.
Rothe	. .	Rōōth.
Rothes	. .	*Roth*-is.
Rothwell	. .	*Row*-ell.
Rouse	. .	Rōōz. / Rouse.
Routh	. .	Rowth.
Rowton	. .	*Rō*-ton.
Roxburghe	.	*Rox*-bra.
Ruislip	. .	*Ry*-slip.
Ruthven	. .	*Riv*-ven.
Rynd	. .	Rind.
Sacheverell	.	Sash-*ev*-erel.
St. Aubyn	.	S'nt *Aw*-bin.
St. Clair	.	*Sin*-clair.
St. Cyres	.	Sin-*seer*.
St. John	.	*Sin*-jun.
St. Leger		*Sil*-linjer. / S'nt *Lej*-er.
St. Maur		S'nt *Mor*. / *See*-mer.
St. Neots	.	S'nt *Neets*.
Salisbury	.	*Sawl*-sberri.
Saltoun		*Sawl*-ton. / *Sal*-ton.
Sandes / Sandys	.	Sands.
Sanquhar	.	*San*-ker.
Sartorius	.	*Sar*-toris.
Satow	.	Sa-*tō*.
Sault-St. Marie	.	Soo-St. Marie.
Saumarez / Sausmarez	.	*So*-marrez.
Saunders	.	*Sahn*-ders.
Saunderson	.	*Sahn*-derson.
Sawbridgeworth		*Sap*-sed (Old). / Modern pronunciation as spelt.
Saye and Sele	.	Say an Seel.
Sayer	. .	Sair.
Scafell	.	*Scaw*-fell.
Scarborough	.	*Scar*-burra.
Scarbrough	.	*Scar*-bra.
Sciennes	.	Sheens.
Sclater	.	*Slay*-ter.
Scone	. .	Scoon.
Scrymgeour	.	*Scrim*-jer.
Searle	. .	Serl.
Sedbergh	.	*Sed*-ber.
Selous	.	Se-*loo*.
Sempill	.	*Semp*-il.
Sergeant	.	*Sar*-jent.
Seton / Setoun	.	*See*-ton.
Seymour	.	*See*-mer.
Shaen	. .	Shane.

Shakerley	.	*Shak*-erli.
Shearman	.	*Sher*-man.
Sherbourne	.	*Sher*-bern.
Shrewsbury	.	*Shrō*-sberri.
Sidebotham	.	*Side*-bottam.
Skrine	.	Skreen.
Slaithwaite	.	*Slo*-it.
Smijth	.	Smythe.
Sodor	.	*So*-dor.
Somers	.	*Sum*-mers.
Somerset	.	*Sum*-erset.
Somerton	.	*Sum*-merton.
Somervell	.	*Sum*-mervle.
Sondes	.	Sonds.
Sotherby	.	*Suth*-ebi.
Southwell	.	*Su*-thell.
Souttar	.	*Soo*-tar.
Speight	.	Spate.
Stalbridge	.	*Stawl*-bridge.
Stanton	.	*Stahn*-ton.
Stapley	.	*Stayp*-li.
Stavordale	.	*Stay*-vordale.
Stormonth	.	*Stor*-munth.
Stoughton	.	{*Staw*-ton. / *Stow*-ton.
Stourton	.	*Ster*-ton.
Strachey	.	*Stray*-shi.
Strahan / Strachan	.	Strawn.
Stranraer	.	Stran-*rar*.
Strathallan	.	Strath-*al*-an.
Strathcona	.	Strath-*co*-na.
Stratheden	.	Strath-*ee*-den.
Strathmore	.	*Strath*-mor.
Straton	.	*Strat*-ton.
Stucley	.	*Stew*-kli.
Sudeley	.	*Sewd*-li.
Sudley	.	*Sud*-li.
Suirdale	.	*Sheur*-dale.
Sweatman	.	*Swet*-man.
Sweetman	.	*Sweet*-man.
Swiney	.	*Swin*-ni.
Symonds	.	*Sim*-monds.
Symons	.	*Sim*-mons.
Synge	.	Sing.

Tangye	.	*Tang*-i.
Teignmouth	.	*Tin*-muth.
Tewkesbury	.	*Tewks*-berri.
Teynham	.	*Tan*-am.
Thames	.	Tems.
Theobald	.	*Tib*-bald.
Thesiger	.	*Thes*-sijer.
Thorold	.	*Thur*-uld.
Thuillier	.	*Twil*-lier.
Thynne	.	Thin.
Tighe	.	Ty.
Tirebuck	.	*Tyre*-buk.
Tollemache	.	*Tol*-mash.
Torphichen	.	Tor-*fick*-en.
Toynbee	.	*Toyn*-bi.
Trafalgar	.	{Tra-*fal*-gar (Square). / Trafal-*gar* (title).
Traquair	.	Trak-*ware*.
Tredegar	.	Tred-*ee*-gar.
Trefusis	.	Tre-*few*-sis.
Treloar	.	Tre-*lor*.
Tremenheere	.	*Trem*-menhear.
Trethewy	.	Tre-*thew*-i.
Trevelyan	.	Tre-*vi*-lian.
Treves	.	Treevs.
Trewin	.	Tre-*win*.
Trimlestown	.	*Trim*-melston.
Trottiscliffe	.	*Tros*-li.
Troubridge	.	*Troo*-bridge.
Tuite	.	Tewt.
Tullibardine	.	Tulli-*bard*-een.
Turnour	.	*Ter*-ner.
Tuttiett	.	*Tut*-yet.
Tyrwhitt	.	*Tir*-rit.
Tyssen	.	*Ty*-sen.
Tytler	.	*Tyt*-ler.
Uig	.	*Oo*-ig.
Uist	.	*Oo*-ist.
Urquhart	.	*Erk*-ert.
Uttoxeter	.	Yew-*tox*-eter.
Vaillant	.	{*Val*-lant. / *Val*-liant.
Valletort	.	*Val*-lytort.

Vanburgh	*Van*-bra.	Whytham	*Wÿte*-am.
Vandam	Van-*dam*.	Wilde	Wyld.
Van Dyck	Van-*dyke*.	Willard	Will-*ard*.
Vaughan	Vawn.	Willes	Wills.
Vaux	Vox. / Vokes.	Willoughby	*Wil*-lobi.
Vavasour	*Vav*-vaser.	Willoughby-D'Eresby	*Wil*-lobi-Dersbi.
Vesey	*Vee*-zi.	Willoughby de Broke	*Wil*-loby de Brook.
Vezin	*Vee*-zin.	Winchilsea	*Winch*-elsee.
Villiers	*Vil*-lers.	Winstanley	*Win*-stanli.
Vogel	*Vo*-gel.	Woburn	*Woo*-bern.
Voules	Voles.	Wodehouse	*Wood*-house.
Vyvyan	*Viv*-vian.	Wolcombe	*Wool*-cum.
		Wollaston	*Wool*-aston.
Waldegrave	*Wawl*-grave.	Wolmer	*Wool*-mer.
Waleran	*Wawl*-ran.	Wolseley	*Wool*-sli.
Walford	*Wawl*-ford.	Wombwell	*Woom*-well.
Wallop	*Wol*-lup.	Woolwich	*Wool*-ich.
Walmesley	*Wawm*-sli.	Worcester	*Woos*-ter.
Walrond	*Wawl*-rund.	Worksop	*Wer*-sup.
Walsingham	*Wawl*-singam.	Worlledge	*Wer*-lij.
Wantage	*Won*-tij.	Worsley	*Wer*-sli.
Warburton	*War*-burton.	Wortley	*Wert*-li.
Warkworth	*Wawk*-werth.	Wraxhall	*Rax*-all.
Warre	Wor.	Wreford	*Ree*-ford.
Warwick	*Wor*-rick.	Wrensfordsley	*Ren*-sli.
Wastell	*Wos*-sel. / *Wos*-tel.	Wrey	Ray.
Wauchope	*Waw*-kup.	Wriothesley	*Ry*-othsli. / *Rox*-li.
Waugh	Waw.	Wrixon	*Rix*-on.
Wavertree	*Waw*-tri.	Wrotham	*Roo*-tham.
Wednesbury	*Wens*-berri.	Wrottesley	*Rot*-sli.
Weguelin	*Weg*-gelin.	Wroughton	*Raw*-ton.
Weir	Weer.	Wylie / Wyllie	*Wÿ*-li.
Wellesley	*Wel*-sli. / *Wes*-li.		
Wemyss	Weems.	Yeames	Yames.
Westcott	*West*-cot.	Yeates	Yayts.
Westenra	*West*-enra.	Yeatman	*Yayt*-man.
Weyman	*Way*-man. / *Wy*-man.	Yeats	Yayts.
Whalley	*Whay*-li.	Yerburgh	*Yar*-burra.
Whichcote	*Wich*-cot.	Yonge / Young	Yung.
Whichelo	*Wich*-elo.	Youghal	Yawl.
Whitefield	*Whit*-field.	Younger	*Yun*-ger.
Whittinghame	*Wit*-enam.		
Whymper	*Wim*-per.	Zouche	Zoosh.

TITLES AND FORMS OF ADDRESS

ROYALTY

Style of Addressing in Speech

On presentation to the Queen the subject does not start the conversation. He or she will answer, using in the first instance the title Your Majesty, and subsequently Ma'am.

For all royal princes the same rules apply, the title used in the first instance being Your Royal Highness, and subsequently Sir. Royal princesses, whether married or unmarried, are called in the first instance Your Royal Highness, and subsequently Ma'am.

Style of Addressing in Writing

THE QUEEN

Madam, *or*
May it please Your Majesty,

> I have the honour to remain, Madam,
> Your Majesty's most humble and obedient subject,

Address of envelope (for formal or State documents only)—
> To The Queen's Most Excellent Majesty,

Otherwise—
> To Her Majesty The Queen.

THE DUKE OF EDINBURGH

is entitled to the style of a Prince of the Blood Royal, as His Royal Highness The Prince Philip, Duke of Edinburgh.

QUEEN MOTHER

Addressing Envelope—

To Her Majesty Queen [Elizabeth the Queen Mother].

Otherwise as for the Queen.

PRINCES AND PRINCESSES OF THE BLOOD ROYAL
DUKES AND DUCHESSES OF THE BLOOD ROYAL

Sir (or Madam),

I have the honour to be, Sir (or Madam),
Your Royal Highness's most humble and obedient servant,

Address of envelope—

To His (or Her) Royal Highness the Prince (or Princess) ——
To His (or Her) Royal Highness the Duke (or Duchess) of ——

A writer not personally known to the Queen or other member of the Royal Family should address his letter to the Private Secretary, Equerry or Lady in Waiting of the person concerned, asking that the subject of the letter be made known to Her Majesty (or to His or Her Royal Highness).

THE PEERAGE

THE peerage has five descending grades. They are DUKES, MARQUESSES, EARLS, VISCOUNTS, and BARONS, and in each grade there are five classes. We will take them all in turn, creating a new title in each grade for our examples.

DOWAGER PEERESSES

These rules apply to the five grades of the peerage and also to the baronetage.

A dowager peeress is the earliest surviving widow of a preceding holder of the title, irrespective of her relationship to the existing holder. She may thus be mother, grandmother, aunt, great-aunt, etc.

Example.—The Dowager Duchess of Middlesex.

Socially, however, a dowager peeress may prefer to be known not as Dowager, but by her Christian name; if this is so, she will probably make an announcement in the press of the style she prefers.

Where a Dowager is alive, succeeding widows use their Christian name.

Example.—Mary, Duchess of Middlesex.

If the existing peer has no wife, the widow of his predecessor usually prefers to be addressed as if her husband were still alive, without prefix or Christian name.

When the Dowager dies, the next senior widow becomes the Dowager.

In Scotland the style of Dowager is applied only where the peeress is mother or grandmother of the reigning peer; it is carefully retained in Scottish families, since it emphasizes that the widow became ancestress of an heir.

FORMER WIVES OF PEERS

The wife of a peer whose marriage has been dissolved uses her Christian name.

Example.—Mary, Duchess of Middlesex.

PEERESSES RE-MARRYING

A peeress who re-marries loses the title she acquired by marriage to a peer; but retains or resumes any title she previously bore in her own right, or as the daughter of a peer.

COURTESY TITLES

All peers have a family name as well as their titles, although in numerous cases, especially in the lower ranks of the peerage, the two are the same. The family name is used by the sons and daughters of peers, excepting in the cases of eldest sons of dukes, marquesses, and earls.

In almost every case peers of these three categories have lesser titles also, of which the eldest son usually takes the highest as his courtesy title and uses it in every way as if it were his by right. In the few cases where there are no second titles, as in the earldoms of Devon, Huntingdon, and Temple of Stowe, the family name is used as a courtesy title. The eldest son of a duke is born in the degree of a marquess, but his courtesy title depends upon his father's lesser dignities. He takes the highest of these, which may be only that of an earl, a viscount, or a baron. He takes his title from birth, and, when he marries, his wife becomes a marchioness or a countess, or whatever it may be, and his children take the titles attached to those ranks. The eldest son of an eldest son takes a third title from the ducal collection, but of a lower grade than that of his father.

The correct ways of using these titles will be found under their various headings. They are in all respects the same, whether they are actual or courtesy titles, except that the prefixes, Most Honourable and Right Honourable, or The (which stands in their place; *see* p. 45), are not used for courtesy titles.

COLLATERALS

All courtesy titles, or titles connected with the family name of a peer, are attached only to the actual descendants of that peer, with one exception, hardly to be called such. It is that when a peer is succeeded other than by a son, the new peer's brothers and sisters may take the titles that would have been theirs if their father had succeeded. In such cases he *would* have succeeded had he lived, so the honour really comes through him. His widow, however, if he has left one, does not share this indulgence.

For instance, the 8th Duke of Devonshire died without issue. His heir was the eldest son of his brother, Lord Edward Cavendish, who had predeceased him. As long as the 8th duke lived his heir presumptive had no title, nor of course had his two brothers. But when Mr Victor Cavendish succeeded to the dukedom, his brothers became Lord Richard and Lord John Cavendish. His mother, however, remained Lady Edward Cavendish.

But it should be clearly understood that these privileges cannot be claimed as a right. They are given by favour of the Crown, and warrants are granted in such cases only upon the recommendation of the Home Secretary.

ADDRESSING THE HEIR ON SUCCESSION

It is customary to continue to address the heir of a

peerage or a baronetcy, when the peer or baronet dies, by the courtesy title or other style by which he was formerly known until after his predecessor's funeral.

LIFE PEERS AND LIFE PEERESSES

Life peers and life peeresses rank with hereditary barons and baronesses according to the date of their creation. Wives of life peers take the title of Lady, and their children The Honourable. Husbands of life peeresses do not take any title. Children of life peeresses, however, take the title The Honourable. In all respects, except that the title does not descend, rules as for BARONS and BARONESSES apply (*see* p. 83).

DISCLAIMING OF HEREDITARY PEERAGES

The Peerage Act of 1963 authorised the disclaimer for life of certain hereditary peerages. A peer who disclaims his peerage loses all titles and precedence attached to it; he cannot however disclaim a baronetcy or a knighthood, and if he possesses one will be known by the appropriate title. His wife also loses the title and precedence which she received from her husband's hereditary peerage, although not, of course, any title and precedence she may herself have possessed. The eldest son of a disclaimed peer may continue if he wishes to use the courtesy title he used previously, and other children to use the titles Lord, Lady or The Honourable.

PEERESSES IN THEIR OWN RIGHT

Some baronies and a few earldoms descend in the female line. A peeress in her own right is addressed exactly as though the rank were obtained through marriage.

HUSBANDS AND CHILDREN OF PEERESSES IN THEIR OWN RIGHT

Husbands take no style or dignity from their wives. Their children, however, are in all respects as if the peerage were held by their father.

HUSBANDS AND CHILDREN OF PEERS' DAUGHTERS

A husband's name or status is not altered in any way by his wife's degree, and the children have no distinctions of any sort through their mother.

DEVOLVING TITLES

A hereditary title descends only in the oldest direct line, that is from father to son, or grandfather to grandson, except in such instances as those already mentioned, in which descent also includes the female line, and those in which remainder is expressly granted. In the case of an ancient peerage, succession sometimes devolves upon a distant cousin, but he succeeds not because he is a cousin of the preceding peer, but because he is descended from some former holder of the title. The brother or nephew of a newly created peer would not succeed to his honours unless special remainder were granted to his Patent, nor would a cousin of an older creation, unless his descent were from a former holder of it. This explains why some peers succeeding take lower titles than their predecessors. The 9th Earl of Drogheda, for instance, gained the title through descent from the fifth earl. The sixth earl was raised to the marquessate, which was held also by the seventh and eighth earls, as his direct descendants. But with the death of the third marquess the direct male descent from the first died out, though descent from previous holders of the lower title did not.

THE PREFIX "THE"

Members of the Peerage are entitled by ancient custom, almost amounting to a right, to the following appellations:

Dukes—The Most Noble.
Marquesses—The Most Honourable.
Other Peers—The Right Honourable.

The practice is not to make use of the full title of Peers when referring to them, but to shorten the prefix to "The" as "The Duke of Norfolk".

The use of "The Lord" is really short for "The Right Hon. Lord". When "Lord" is used without a prefix it is for a courtesy title.

Where any Peer is entitled to the additional prefix of Right Honourable by virtue of a Privy Counsellorship (*see* p. 112), the addition merges in that attaching to the existing title; but Dukes and Marquesses retain the right to both their designations in legal documents and formal circumstances. "The Right Hon." should not be shortened to "The" (as above) when a Peer is also a Privy Counsellor; his membership of the Privy Council entitles him to the full prefix at all times. Membership of the Privy Council being an office and not an honour, the initials P.C. should not be appended to any name or title.

THE TITLE "LADY"

This is probably the commonest of all, as it is used of all peeresses under the rank of duchess, of all daughters of the three highest ranks of the peerage, and of the wives of baronets and knights. The prefix "The" was once by general custom used in addressing the daughters of dukes, marquesses and earls, e.g. "The Lady Jean Smith". The practice existed only by courtesy, and was not recognized as correct by, for example, the College of Arms; it is no longer generally used, although it would be wrong to deprive elderly ladies of the prefix should they feel strongly about it. Ladies do not retain their husbands' titles on re-marriage to commoners.

THE TITLE "HONOURABLE"

This title is a fairly frequent one, including as it does the younger sons of earls, all the sons and daughters of viscounts and barons, and the wives of the sons, besides its use outside the ranks of the peerage. The important rule to note is that it is *never* used in speech, even by a servant. Neither is it used in letter-writing, except on the envelope. (*See also* p. 157, for uses outside the peerage.)

TERRITORIAL ADDITIONS

All peerages have still, as in their origin, a territorial basis, which is expressed in the Letters Patent creating a new peerage, as BARON SMITH, of (a place with which the new Baron has connections) in the County of —————. This, which may be described as the "address" of the peerage, does not form part of the title, and should never be used as though it did. Some peerages, however, have a territorial addition included in their titles, to avoid confusion with older peerages of the same name (whether or not these still survive). In these cases, of which the Baronies of Morris, Morris of Borth-y-Gest, Morris of Grasmere, and Morris of Kenwood make a good example, the Letters Patent will read e.g. BARON MORRIS OF GRASMERE, of Grasmere in the County of Westmorland, and it will be clear that the territorial addition forms part of the title, and should be used in addressing or referring to the peer. It is not possible for peers to change their titles from the form in which they were first created.

(*See also* p. 104 for the Scottish use of territorial additions.)

DUKES AND DUCHESSES

To help us in our explanation we will create a Duke of Middlesex, who is also Marquess of Huddersfield and Earl of Ramsgate, to name only his principal titles. His family name shall be Smith.

The titles of all existing dukedoms are taken from the name of a place. (There are no instances of the title being taken from the family name. In those cases where the two are the same, the family name has been taken from the place.)

> *Example.*—The Duke of Middlesex.
> The Duchess of Middlesex.

Style of Addressing in Speech

The formal style of a Duke is "The Most Noble the Duke of . . .", but the form of address for those of social equality is Duke of Middlesex or Duchess of Middlesex, though the necessity for using the full title would generally be avoided. For instance, if there is no need to distinguish between different dukes and duchesses, plain Duke or Duchess is correct. They are referred to as The Duke or The Duchess. But in conversation it is best to make as sparing a use as possible of titles. Formally addressed as Your Grace, they are referred to as His Grace and Her Grace.

The archaic style of the title in conjunction with a Christian name, as Duke John, is not now used. To distinguish a particular duke from others of his line he is called John, Duke of————, or The second Duke of ————.

A dowager duchess is so called when she is the earliest surviving widow of a preceding duke irrespective of her relationship to the reigning duke (but *see* p. 40 for

47

Scottish practice). Later surviving widows are distinguished by the use of their Christian name before the title (*see* p. 40).

> *Examples.*—The Dowager Duchess of Middlesex.
> Mary, Duchess of Middlesex.

But if the existing duke has no wife, the widow of his predecessor is addressed in all respects as if her husband were alive.

> *Example.*—The Duchess of Middlesex.

The rules for addressing in speech are in all ways the same as for the duke's wife, but if confusion were threatened she would be referred to as The Dowager Duchess.

Style of Addressing in Writing

The most formal manner of address in writing is:

My Lord Duke,

> I remain,
> Your Grace's most obedient servant,

Address of envelope—
> His Grace The Duke of Middlesex.

Madam,

> I remain,
> Your Grace's most obedient servant,

Address of envelope—
> Her Grace The Duchess of Middlesex.

Less formally, but still not socially:

My Lord Duke,
> Yours faithfully,

Address of envelope—
> His Grace The Duke of Middlesex.

Madam,
                    Yours faithfully,

Address of envelope—
     Her Grace The Duchess of Middlesex.

                    (*To a Dowager.*)
Madam,
                         I remain,
                    Your Grace's most obedient servant,

    or—
Madam,
                    Yours faithfully.

Address of envelope—
     Her Grace The Dowager Duchess of Middlesex,   *or*
     Her Grace Mary, Duchess of Middlesex.

                    (*To a Former Wife.*)
Madam,
                         I remain, Madam,
                    Your most obedient servant,

    or—
Madam,
                    Yours faithfully,

Address of envelope—
     Mary, Duchess of Middlesex.

The social manner of address in writing is:
Dear Duke of Middlesex,
                    Yours sincerely,

                    or more familiarly
Dear Duke,
                    Yours sincerely,

Address of envelope—
     His Grace The Duke of Middlesex.

Dear Duchess of Middlesex,
                    Yours sincerely,

or more familiarly

Dear Duchess,

Yours sincerely,

Address of envelope—

Her Grace The Duchess of Middlesex.

(*To a Dowager.*)

Dear Duchess of Middlesex,

Yours sincerely,

or more familiarly

Dear Duchess,

Yours sincerely,

Address of envelope—

Her Grace The Dowager Duchess of Middlesex,

or

Her Grace Mary, Duchess of Middlesex.

In social address the prefix His Grace or Her Grace may be omitted from the envelope.

(*To a Former Wife.*)

Dear Duchess of Middlesex,

Yours sincerely,

or more familiarly

Dear Duchess,

Yours sincerely,

Address of envelope—

Mary, Duchess of Middlesex.

ELDEST SONS OF DUKES

(*See also under* COURTESY TITLES, p. 41)

The eldest son of a duke is born in the degree of a marquess, but his courtesy title depends upon his father's lesser dignities. He normally takes the highest of these, which may be only that of an earl or lesser degree. He takes his title from birth, and, when he marries, his wife and children share the honours attached to his rank. His eldest son takes a third title from the ducal collection, of a lower grade than that of his father.

Example.—The eldest son of our Duke of Middlesex would be Marquess of Huddersfield and his wife Marchioness of Huddersfield. Their eldest son would be Earl of Ramsgate.

The correct use of these titles will be found under their various headings. It is in all respects the same, whether they are actual or courtesy titles, except that the prefix Most Honourable, or "The", which represents it, is not used, i.e. Marquess of Huddersfield, not The Most Honourable The Marquess of Huddersfield. (*See* pp. 41 and 45.)

DAUGHTERS AND YOUNGER SONS OF DUKES

The younger sons of a duke bear the title "Lord" with their Christian and family names, and all daughters of a duke bear the title "Lady".

> *Example.*—Lord John Smith.
> Lady Barbara Smith.

STYLE OF ADDRESSING IN SPEECH

In this category the commonest mistakes are made by those who do not know the distinctions between the sorts of people who are entitled to be called "Lord" or "Lady". Lord John Smith must *never* be called Lord Smith, nor Lady Barbara Smith Lady Smith. When the full titles are not used they are called Lord John and Lady Barbara. There is no other abbreviation unless one is on such terms of intimacy as to use their Christian names alone, or, in the case of the men, their surnames alone.

The most formal manner of address in writing is:

My Lord,
>> I have the honour to remain,
>>> Your Lordship's obedient servant,

Address of envelope—
> Lord John Smith.

My Lady (or Madam),
>> I have the honour to remain,
>>> Your Ladyship's obedient servant,

Address of envelope—
> Lady Barbara Smith.

Less formally, but still not socially:

My Lord,
>> Yours faithfully,

Address of envelope—
> Lord John Smith.

Madam,
>> Yours faithfully,

Address of envelope—
> Lady Barbara Smith.

The social manner of address in writing is:

Dear Lord John Smith,
>> Yours sincerely,

>> *or more familiarly*

Dear Lord John,
>> Yours sincerely, *or*

Dear Smith,
>> Yours sincerely,

Address of envelope—
> Lord John Smith.

Dear Lady Barbara Smith,
> Yours sincerely,

> *or more familiarly*

Dear Lady Barbara,
> Yours sincerely,

Address of envelope—
> Lady Barbara Smith.

WIVES OF YOUNGER SONS OF DUKES

The mistake already alluded to in this category is made most often of all in the case of wives of younger sons of dukes and marquesses. The wife of Lord John Smith is Lady John Smith, and never in any circumstances Lady Smith. She is known less formally as Lady John. This rule is varied only when she is of higher rank than her husband, in which case her own Christian name is substituted for his. (*See under* MARRIED DAUGHTERS OF DUKES, p. 54.)

STYLE OF ADDRESSING IN WRITING

The most formal manner is:

Madam (or My Lady),
> I have the honour to remain,
> > Your Ladyship's obedient servant,

Address of envelope—
> Lady John Smith.

Less formally, but still not socially:
Madam,
> Yours faithfully,

5

Address of envelope—
          Lady John Smith.

The social manner of address in writing is:

Dear Lady John Smith,
                    Yours sincerely,

              or more familiarly

Dear Lady John,
                    Yours sincerely,

    Address of envelope—
          Lady John Smith.

WIDOWS OF YOUNGER SONS OF DUKES

If the widow of a younger son of a duke, having no title of her own, re-marries, she may not continue to use her late husband's name and title. If, on the other hand, she has a title of her own, she will use it coupled with her new name. If she re-marries into the peerage, she will obviously share her second husband's name and title. The same rules apply to former wives as to widows.

CHILDREN OF YOUNGER SONS OF DUKES

The children of younger sons of dukes have no distinctions of any sort. All the sons and daughters of Lord and Lady John Smith would be plain Mr or Miss. A popular fallacy would make them honourables, but that is quite wrong. They have, of course, some precedence in the social scale.

MARRIED DAUGHTERS OF DUKES

The daughter of a duke, in marrying a peer (not a courtesy peer), shares her husband's title and precedence.

In all other cases she retains her own title of Lady with her Christian name even if she marries the younger son of a duke, because by a curious anomaly all peers' daughters rank one degree higher than younger sons of the same grade. In the event of marriage with the heir of an earl or lesser peer, she is entitled, if she prefers it, to retain her own title while her husband is a courtesy lord, because she actually keeps her precedence until he succeeds to his peerage. There are instances of both usages in the peerage, and the chosen style should be ascertained in each case. Marriage with a commoner does not alter her rank in any way (nor, incidentally, that of her husband). Our duke's daughter, Lady Barbara Smith, married to Mr Peter Green, would become Lady Barbara Green. In no circumstances would she be called Lady Peter Green. Together they would be referred to as Mr Peter and Lady Barbara Green, or Mr and Lady Barbara Green. Curiously enough, however, the daughter of a duke (as also of a marquess or earl) keeps her rank as such in the table of precedence if she marries out of the peerage, but exchanges it for that of her husband if she remains in it, even if it means descending several steps. Thus Lady Barbara, having married Mr Peter Green, would go in to dinner before a sister who had married a baron.

Examples.—Marriage with

A commoner	Peter Green, Esq.	Lady Barbara Green
Scottish chief or laird	James MacBrown of Glenbrown	Lady Barbara MacBrown of Glenbrown
A knight or baronet	Sir Bernard Brown	Lady Barbara Brown
A younger son of an earl or lesser peer	The Honourable George Wilson	Lady Barbara Wilson
An eldest son of an earl	Viscount Staines (Lord Staines)	Lady Barbara Staines, *or* Viscountess Staines (Lady Staines), as she prefers

A younger son of a duke or marquess	Lord John Bull	Lady Barbara Bull
An eldest son of a marquess	Earl of Malvern (Lord Malvern)	Countess of Malvern (Lady Malvern) *or* Lady Barbara Malvern, as she prefers
An eldest son of a duke	Marquess of Mere (Lord Mere)	Marchioness of Mere (Lady Mere)
A peer of any rank	The Right Hon. Lord Slough (The Lord Slough)	The Right Hon . Lady Slough (The Lady Slough)

CHILDREN OF DAUGHTERS OF DUKES

The children of daughters of dukes receive no titles or distinctions of any sort through their mother.

MARQUESSES AND MARCHIONESSES

THIS title is rendered in two ways, marquess or marquis. The former is the older and purely British. Peers of this rank use which form they prefer, and their choice should be ascertained and observed in addressing them.

Our typical peer of this, the second grade, shall be the Marquess of Montgomeryshire, who is also the Earl of Malvern and Baron Swindon. His family name shall be Evans.

TERRITORIAL TITLES

The title of marquess is generally taken from the name of a place, as it invariably is in the case of a duke.

Example.—The Marquess of Montgomeryshire.

There are two marquessates in our peerage, however, whose titles are taken from the family names, and in both these cases the preposition is dropped, thus:

The Marquess Conyngham.
The Marquess Townshend.

These two are the only instances in the marquessate of titles taken from family names, but in two other cases the preposition is dropped even though the titles are territorial, viz.,

The Marquess Camden.
The Marquess Douro.

STYLE OF ADDRESSING IN SPEECH

It has been said already that all peers and peeresses below ducal rank are called lord and lady in speech.

This brings us to a mistake quite commonly made in connection with the lower grades of the peerage. Although it is correct to talk of The Duke, or Duchess, of Middlesex —indeed, they could not be referred to in any other way —the rule is quite different for the marquessate. The Marquess and Marchioness of Montgomeryshire would always be referred and spoken to as Lord and Lady Montgomeryshire. There are a few formal occasions on which the full title would be used, but it would never occur in intimate speech.

STYLE OF ADDRESSING IN WRITING

The most formal manner is:

My Lord Marquess,   *or*
My Lord,

> I have the honour to be,
>> Your Lordship's obedient servant,

Address of envelope—
The Most Hon. The Marquess of Montgomeryshire.

Madam,

> I have the honour to remain,
>> Your Ladyship's obedient servant,

Address of envelope—
The Most Hon. The Marchioness of Montgomeryshire.

Less formally, but still not socially:

My Lord,

> Yours faithfully,

Address of envelope—
The Most Hon. The Marquess of Montgomeryshire.

Madam,

> Yours faithfully,

Address of envelope—
The Most Hon. The Marchioness of Montgomeryshire.

The social manner of address in writing is:

Dear Lord Montgomeryshire,   *or*
Dear Montgomeryshire,

> Yours sincerely,

Address of envelope—
> The Marquess of Montgomeryshire.

Dear Lady Montgomeryshire,

> Yours sincerely,

Address of envelope—
> The Marchioness of Montgomeryshire.

DOWAGER MARCHIONESSES

A dowager marchioness is so called when she is the earliest surviving widow of a preceding marquess, irrespective of her relationship to the reigning marquess (but *see* p. 40 for Scottish practice). A later surviving widow is distinguished by the use of her Christian name before her title (*see* p. 40).

Examples.—The Dowager Marchioness of Montgomeryshire.
> Enid, Marchioness of Montgomeryshire.

STYLE OF ADDRESSING IN WRITING

The most formal manner is:

Madam,
> I have the honour to remain,
> > Your Ladyship's obedient servant,

Less formally:

Madam,
> Yours faithfully,

Address of envelope—
The Most Hon. The Dowager Marchioness of Montgomeryshire,   *or*

The Most Hon. Enid, Marchioness of Montgomeryshire.

The social manner of address in writing is:

Dear Lady Montgomeryshire,

Yours sincerely,

Address of envelope—
>   The Dowager Marchioness of Montgomeryshire,   *or*
>   Enid, Marchioness of Montgomeryshire.

The former wife of a Marquess uses her Christian name before the title.

STYLE OF ADDRESSING IN WRITING

The most formal manner is:

Madam,

I have the honour to remain,
Your Ladyship's obedient servant,

Less formally:

Madam,

Yours faithfully,

Address of envelope (in each case)—
>   Enid, Marchioness of Montgomeryshire.

The social manner of address in writing is:

Dear Lady Montgomeryshire,

Yours sincerely,

Address of envelope—
>   Enid, Marchioness of Montgomeryshire.

ELDEST SONS OF MARQUESSES
(See also under COURTESY TITLES, p. 41)

As stated elsewhere, peers in this category have lesser titles as well, and the eldest son takes usually the highest of these as his courtesy title, which is used in every way as if it were his by right. He takes the title from birth, and on his marriage his wife and children share the honours attached to his rank. His eldest son would take a third title from among the marquess's lesser titles.

Example.—The eldest son of our Marquess of Montgomeryshire would be Earl of Malvern and his wife Countess of Malvern. Their eldest son would be Baron Swindon. The correct use of these titles will be found under their various headings. It is in all respects the same, whether they are actual or courtesy titles, except that the prefix Right Honourable, or "The", which represents it, is not used, i.e.

Earl of Malvern (See pp. 41 and 45.)

DAUGHTERS AND YOUNGER SONS OF MARQUESSES

The younger sons of a marquess bear the title Lord with their Christian and family names, and all daughters of a marquess bear the title Lady.

Example.—Lord Charles Evans.
Lady Joan Evans.

Style of Addressing in Speech

In this category the commonest mistakes are made. Lord Charles Evans must never be called Lord Evans nor Lady Joan Evans Lady Evans. When the full titles are not used, they are called Lord Charles and Lady Joan. There is no other abbreviation.

Style of Addressing in Writing

The most formal manner of address in writing is:

My Lord,
>> I have the honour to remain,
>>> Your Lordship's obedient servant,

> *Address of envelope—*
>> Lord Charles Evans.

Madam (or My Lady),
>> I have the honour to remain,
>>> Your Ladyship's obedient servant,

> *Address of envelope—*
>> Lady Joan Evans.

Less formally, but still not socially:

My Lord,
>> Yours faithfully,

> *Address of envelope—*
>> Lord Charles Evans.

Madam,
>> Yours faithfully,

> *Address of envelope—*
>> Lady Joan Evans.

The social manner of address in writing is:

Dear Lord Charles Evans,
>> Yours sincerely,

>> *or more familiarly*

Dear Lord Charles,

or

Dear Evans,
>> Yours sincerely,

> *Address of envelope—*
>> Lord Charles Evans.

Dear Lady Joan Evans,

> Yours sincerely,

> *or more familiarly*

Dear Lady Joan,

> Yours sincerely,

Address of envelope—

> Lady Joan Evans.

WIVES OF YOUNGER SONS OF MARQUESSES

The mistake already alluded to in this category is made most often of all in the case of wives of younger sons of dukes and marquesses. The wife of Lord Charles Evans is Lady Charles Evans, and never in any circumstances Lady Evans. She is known less formally as Lady Charles. This rule is varied only when she is of higher rank than her husband, in which case her own Christian name is substituted for his. (*See under* MARRIED DAUGHTERS OF MARQUESSES, p. 64.)

STYLE OF ADDRESSING IN WRITING

The most formal manner is:

Madam (or My Lady),

> I have the honour to remain,
> > Your Ladyship's obedient servant,

Address of envelope—

> Lady Charles Evans.

Less formally:

Madam,

> Yours faithfully,

Address of envelope—

> Lady Charles Evans.

The social manner of address in writing is:

Dear Lady Charles Evans,

Yours sincerely,

or more familiarly

Dear Lady Charles,

Yours sincerely,

Address of envelope—

Lady Charles Evans.

WIDOWS OF YOUNGER SONS OF MARQUESSES

If the widow of a younger son of a marquess, having no title of her own, re-marries she may not continue to use her late husband's name and title. If, on the other hand, she has a title of her own, she will use it coupled with her new name. The same rules apply to former wives as to widows.

CHILDREN OF YOUNGER SONS OF MARQUESSES

The children of younger sons of marquesses have no distinctions of any sort. All the sons and daughters of Lord and Lady Charles Evans would be plain Mr and Miss. They have, of course, some precedence in the social scale.

MARRIED DAUGHTERS OF MARQUESSES

The daughter of a marquess, in marrying a peer (not a courtesy peer), shares her husband's title and precedence, as also if she marries a man of equal or higher rank than her own—the eldest son of a marquess or any son of a duke. In all other cases she retains her own title of Lady with her Christian name, even if she marries the younger son of a marquess, because, as stated elsewhere, all peers' daughters rank one degree higher than younger sons of the same grade. In the event of marriage with the heir of an earl or lesser peer, she is entitled, if she prefers it, to retain her own title while her husband is a courtesy lord, because she actually keeps her precedence until he succeeds to his peerage. There are instances of both usages in the peerage, and the chosen style should be ascertained in each case. Marriage with a commoner does not alter her rank in any way (nor, incidentally, that of her husband). Our marquess's daughter, married to Mr Peter Green, would become Lady Joan Green. In no circumstances would she be called Lady Peter Green. Together they would be described as Mr Peter and Lady Joan Green. Curiously enough, however, the daughter of a marquess (as also of a duke or earl) keeps her rank as such in the table of precedence if she marries out of the peerage, but exchanges it for that of her husband if she remains in it, even if it means descending several steps. Thus Lady Joan, having married Mr Peter Green, would go in to dinner before a sister who had married a baron.

Examples.—Marriage with

A commoner	Peter Green, Esq.	Lady Joan Green
A knight or baronet	Sir Bernard Brown	Lady Joan Brown
A younger son of an earl or lesser peer	The Honourable George Wilson	Lady Joan Wilson
An eldest son of an earl	Viscount Staines (Lord Staines)	Lady Joan Staines, *or* Viscountess Staines (Lady Staines), as she prefers
A younger son of a marquess	Lord John Bull	Lady Joan Bull
A younger son of a duke	Lord John Smith	Lady John Smith, *or* Lady Joan Smith, as she prefers

An eldest son of a marquess	Earl of Malvern (Lord Malvern)	Countess of Malvern (Lady Malvern)
An eldest son of a duke	Marquess of Mere (Lord Mere)	Marchioness of Mere (Lady Mere)
A peer of any rank	The Right Hon. Lord Slough (The Lord Slough)	The Right Hon. Lady Slough (The Lady Slough)

CHILDREN OF DAUGHTERS OF MARQUESSES

The children of daughters of marquesses receive no titles or distinctions of any sort through their mother.

EARLS AND COUNTESSES

THIS grade is sometimes territorial, sometimes taken from the family name. In the former case the preposition "of" is generally used, and in the latter case it is not, although there are numerous exceptions to both rules.

In one or two instances, such as the Earl of Winchilsea and Nottingham, two separate earldoms have become merged. Both titles are used on all formal occasions and even on the social envelope. But in social speech and letters only the first one is employed. The Earl of Winchilsea and Nottingham's title provides an instance of the little traps which are sometimes, almost perversely it would seem, set for the unwary. The name of the ancient town from which Lord Winchilsea takes his title is spelt Winchelsea. Another curious instance is that the town of Beaconsfield, from which Disraeli took his title, is pronounced Beckonsfield. He lived within a few miles of it at Hughenden, and must have been aware of this. But his title was pronounced by him as it is written, and continues to be so pronounced.

Our typical peer in this, the third grade, shall be the Earl of Whitby, with a second title, Viscount Staines, and the family name of Collins.

STYLE OF ADDRESSING IN SPEECH

It has been remarked already that all peers and peeresses below ducal rank are called lord and lady in speech. This rule applies, of course, to earls and countesses, who are always referred and spoken to as lord and lady. As in the case of the marquessate, there are a few formal occasions on which the full title would be used, but it would never happen in intimate speech.

The most formal manner is:

My Lord,
> I have the honour to remain,
>> Your Lordship's obedient servant,

Address of envelope—
> The Right Hon. The Earl of Whitby.

Madam,
> I have the honour to remain,
>> Your Ladyship's obedient servant,

Address of envelope—
> The Right Hon. The Countess of Whitby.

Less formally, but still not socially:

My Lord,
> Yours faithfully,

Address of envelope—
> The Right Hon. The Earl of Whitby

Madam,
> Yours faithfully,

Address of envelope—
> The Right Hon. The Countess of Whitby.

The social manner of address in writing is:

Dear Lord Whitby,   *or*
Dear Whitby,
> Yours sincerely,

Address of envelope—
> The Earl of Whitby.

Dear Lady Whitby,
> Yours sincerely,

Address of envelope—
> The Countess of Whitby.

DOWAGER COUNTESSES

A dowager countess is so called when she is the earliest surviving widow of a preceding earl (but *see* p. 40 for Scottish practice). A later surviving widow is distinguished by the use of the Christian name before her title (*see* p. 40).

> The Dowager Countess of Whitby.
> Muriel, Countess of Whitby.

STYLE OF ADDRESSING IN SPEECH
is exactly the same as if she were the reigning countess.

STYLE OF ADDRESSING IN WRITING

The most formal manner is:

Madam,
> I have the honour to remain,
> > Your Ladyship's obedient servant,

Less formally:

Madam,
> Yours faithfully,

Address of envelope—
The Right Hon. The Dowager Countess of Whitby, *or*
The Right Hon. Muriel, Countess of Whitby.

The social manner of address in writing is:

Dear Lady Whitby,
> Yours sincerely,

Address of envelope—
> The Dowager Countess of Whitby, *or*
> Muriel, Countess of Whitby.

The former wife of an Earl uses her Christian name before the title.

The most formal manner is:

Madam,

> I have the honour to remain,
>> Your Ladyship's obedient servant,

Less formally:

Madam,

> Yours faithfully,

Address of envelope—
> Muriel, Countess of Whitby.

The social manner of address in writing is:

Dear Lady Whitby,

> Yours sincerely,

Address of envelope—
> Muriel, Countess of Whitby.

ELDEST SONS OF EARLS

(*See also under* COURTESY TITLES, p. 41)

As stated elsewhere, peers in this category have lesser titles as well, and the eldest son takes usually the highest of these as his courtesy title, which is used in every way as if it were his by right. He takes the title from birth, and on his marriage his wife and children share the honours attached to his rank.

Example.—The eldest son of our Earl of Whitby would be Viscount Staines and his wife Viscountess Staines. The correct use of these titles will be found under their various headings. It is in all respects the same whether they are actual or courtesy titles, with the exception that the prefix Right Honourable, or "The", which represents it, is not used, i.e. Viscount Staines. (*See* pp. 42 and 45.)

DAUGHTERS OF EARLS

Daughters of earls bear the title Lady with their Christian and family names.

Example.—Lady Violet Collins.

STYLE OF ADDRESSING IN SPEECH

The same rules apply as in the case of daughters of dukes and marquesses, viz. when the full title is not used, our earl's daughter will be called Lady Violet. There is no other abbreviation unless one is on such terms of intimacy as to use the Christian name alone.

STYLE OF ADDRESSING IN WRITING

The most formal manner is:

Madam (or My Lady),
  I have the honour to remain,
    Your Ladyship's obedient servant,

Less formally:

Madam,
      Yours faithfully,

Address of envelope—
    Lady Violet Collins.

The social manner of address in writing is:

Dear Lady Violet Collins,
      Yours sincerely,

or more familiarly

Dear Lady Violet,

Yours sincerely,

Address of envelope—

Lady Violet Collins.

YOUNGER SONS OF EARLS

Unlike the higher grades of the peerage, younger sons of earls are styled Honourable with their Christian and family names (not initials), and there is nothing to distinguish them from the sons of viscounts and barons.

Example.—The Honourable Thomas Collins.

Style of Addressing in Speech

As remarked elsewhere, this title is never used in speech or letter-writing, excepting on the envelope. The younger sons of earls are called Mr, always in conjunction with the Christian name.

Example.—Mr Thomas Collins.

The title is never printed on visiting-cards, so that without inner knowledge it is difficult to recognize the rank. When it is desired to indicate it, however, a reference to the holder's parentage would be permissible. Servants would announce the younger son of an earl as Mr Thomas Collins.

Style of Addressing in Writing

The most formal manner is:

Sir,

I have the honour to be,

Your obedient servant,

Less formally:

Dear Sir,

Yours faithfully,

Address of envelope—
The Hon. Thomas Collins.

The social manner of address in writing is:

Dear Mr Collins, *or*
Dear Collins,

Yours sincerely,

Address of envelope—
The Hon. Thomas Collins.

WIVES OF YOUNGER SONS OF EARLS

share their husbands' title.

Example.—The Hon. Mrs Thomas Collins.

It should be carefully noted that whereas it is wrong to use the designations Mr or Miss with this title, it is right to use the designation Mrs with it. The title is never used in speech, even by a servant, and the wife of Mr Thomas Collins is always alluded to as Mrs Thomas Collins. If she happens to be of higher rank than her husband, she would use her own title in conjunction with her husband's name—*without the Honourable.*

Style of Addressing in Writing

The most formal manner is:

Madam,

I have the honour to remain,
Your obedient servant,

Less formally:

Dear Madam,

Yours faithfully,

Address of envelope—
> The Hon. Mrs Thomas Collins.

The social manner of address in writing is:

Dear Mrs Collins,

> Yours sincerely,

Address of envelope—
> The Hon. Mrs Thomas Collins.

WIDOWS OF YOUNGER SONS OF EARLS

keep their title until re-marriage, when it is abandoned in favour of the second husband's status, whether it be higher or lower. If the widow possesses a title in her own right she will of course continue to use it. The same rules apply to former wives as to widows, except that it is usual for a former wife to substitute her own Christian name for her former husband's, e.g.

> The Hon. Mrs. Rhoda Collins.

CHILDREN OF YOUNGER SONS OF EARLS

have no distinctions of any sort. They have, of course, certain social precedence.

MARRIED DAUGHTERS OF EARLS

The daughter of an earl, if she marries a peer (not a courtesy peer), or a man of equal or higher rank than her own, shares her husband's title and precedence. Otherwise she retains her own title of Lady with her Christian name, even if she marries the younger son of an earl, because, as stated elsewhere, all peers' daughters rank one degree higher than younger sons of the same grade. In the event of marriage with the heir of a viscount or lesser peer, she is entitled, if she prefers it, to retain her own title until her husband succeeds to his peerage, because she actually keeps her own precedence until then.

In such a case the chosen style should be ascertained. Marriage with a commoner does not alter her rank in any way—nor, incidentally, that of her husband. Our earl's daughter, married to Mr Peter Green, would become Lady Violet Green. She must never be called Lady Peter Green. Together they would be described as Mr Peter and Lady Violet Green. Curiously enough, however, the daughter of an earl keeps her rank as such in the table of precedence if she marries out of the peerage, but exchanges it for that of her husband if she remains in it, even if it means descending several steps. Thus Lady Violet, having married Mr Peter Green would go in to dinner before a sister who had married a baron.

Examples.—Marriage with

A commoner	Mr Peter Green	Lady Violet Green
A knight or baronet	Sir Bernard Brown	Lady Violet Brown
A younger son of an earl or lesser peer	The Honourable Michael O'Mara	Lady Violet O'Mara
An eldest son of an earl	Viscount Staines (Lord Staines)	Viscountess Staines (Lady Staines)
A younger son of a marquess	Lord John Bull	Lady John Bull
A younger son of a duke	Lord John Smith	Lady John Smith
An eldest son of a marquess	Earl of Malvern (Lord Malvern)	Countess of Malvern (Lady Malvern)
An eldest son of a duke	Marquess of Mere (Lord Mere)	Marchioness of Mere (Lady Mere)
A peer of any rank	The Right Hon. Lord Slough (The Lord Slough)	The Right Hon. Lady Slough (The Lady Slough)

CHILDREN OF DAUGHTERS OF EARLS

The children of daughters of earls receive no titles or distinctions of any sort through their mother.

VISCOUNTS AND VISCOUNTESSES

THIS title is sometimes territorial, sometimes derived from the family name, but in neither case is the preposition "of" used between the style and the title, e.g. Viscount Hereford, not The Viscount of Hereford. Viscounts in the peerage of Scotland (or before 1707) *do* include the "of", e.g. The Viscount of Arbuthnott. A number of Viscounts recently created also contain a territorial addition to the title, e.g. Viscount Grey of Fallodon. In such cases the full style is used on formal occasions and in addressing all letters, formal and social.

Our example in this, the fourth grade of the peerage, shall be Viscount O'Mara, with the same family name.

STYLE OF ADDRESSING IN SPEECH

The rule already explained, that all peers and peeresses below ducal rank are called lord and lady in speech, applies equally, of course, to viscounts and their wives. As in other ranks, there are a few formal occasions on which the full title would be used, but it would never happen in intimate speech.

STYLE OF ADDRESSING IN WRITING

The most formal manner is:

My Lord,

I have the honour to remain,

Your Lordship's obedient servant,

Address of envelope—

The Right Hon. The Viscount O'Mara.

Madam,

I have the honour to remain,

Your Ladyship's obedient servant,

Address of envelope—
>The Right Hon. The Viscountess O'Mara.

Less formally, but still not socially:

My Lord,

>>Yours faithfully,

Address of envelope—
>The Right Hon. The Viscount O'Mara.

Madam,

>>Yours faithfully,

Address of envelope—
>The Right Hon. The Viscountess O'Mara.

The social manner of address in writing is:

Dear Lord O'Mara,   *or*
Dear O'Mara,

>>Yours sincerely,

Address of envelope—
>>The Viscount O'Mara.

Dear Lady O'Mara,

>>Yours sincerely,

Address of envelope—
>>The Viscountess O'Mara.

DOWAGER VISCOUNTESSES

A dowager viscountess is the earliest surviving widow of a preceding peer (but *see* p. 40 for the Scottish practice). Later surviving widows are distinguished by the use of the Christian name before the title (*see* p. 40).

STYLE OF ADDRESSING IN SPEECH
is exactly the same as if she were the reigning viscountess (*see above*).

Style of Addressing in Writing

The most formal manner is:

Madam,

I have the honour to remain,

Your Ladyship's obedient servant,

Less formally:

Madam,

Yours faithfully,

Address of envelope—
The Right Hon. The Dowager Viscountess O'Mara,
or
The Right Hon. Anne, Viscountess O'Mara.

The social manner of address in writing is:

Dear Lady O'Mara,

Yours sincerely,

Address of envelope—
The Dowager Viscountess O'Mara,   *or*
Anne, Viscountess O'Mara.

The former wife of a Viscount uses her Christian name before the title.

Style of Addressing in Writing

The most formal manner is:

Madam,

I have the honour to remain,

Your Ladyship's obedient servant,

Less formally:

Madam,

Yours faithfully,

Address of envelope—
Anne, Viscountess O'Mara.

The social manner of address in writing is:

Dear Lady O'Mara,

                  Yours sincerely,

   Address of envelope—

              Anne, Viscountess O'Mara.

ELDEST SONS OF VISCOUNTS

Courtesy titles cease at the grade of an earl, so that the eldest son of a viscount does not take his father's second title, even if he happens to have one. Like his younger brothers, he is merely The Honourable, and his wife shares the title.

       Example.—The Hon. Michael O'Mara.

                The Hon. Mrs O'Mara.

Their visiting-cards would be inscribed "Mr O'Mara" and "Mrs O'Mara" without the Christian name.

STYLE OF ADDRESSING IN SPEECH

As explained before, the title Honourable is never used in speech, so that the eldest son of our viscount would be spoken and referred to as Mr O'Mara and his wife as Mrs O'Mara. This rule is followed by servants also.

STYLE OF ADDRESSING IN WRITING

The most formal manner is:

Sir,

          I have the honour to remain,

                 Your obedient servant,

   Less formally:

Dear Sir,

               Yours faithfully,

   Address of envelope—

           The Hon. Michael O'Mara.

Madam,
> I have the honour to remain,
>> Your obedient servant,

Less formally:

Dear Madam,
> Yours faithfully,

Address of envelope—
> The Hon. Mrs O'Mara.

The social manner of address in writing is:

Dear Mr O'Mara,   *or*
Dear O'Mara,
> Yours sincerely,

Address of envelope—
> The Hon. Michael O'Mara.

Dear Mrs O'Mara,
> Yours sincerely,

Address of envelope—
> The Hon. Mrs O'Mara.

WIDOWS OF ELDEST SONS OF VISCOUNTS

keep their title until re-marriage, when it is abandoned in favour of the second husband's status, whether it be higher or lower. This does not apply, of course, if the widow possesses a title in her own right. The same rules apply to former wives as to widows, except that it is usual for a former wife to insert her own Christian name, eg.

> The Hon. Mrs Helen O'Mara.

YOUNGER SONS OF VISCOUNTS
WIVES OF YOUNGER SONS OF VISCOUNTS
WIDOWS OF YOUNGER SONS OF VISCOUNTS
FORMER WIVES OF YOUNGER SONS OF
VISCOUNTS

The same rules exactly apply here as to younger sons of earls and their wives (*see* pp. 72 and 73).

DAUGHTERS OF VISCOUNTS

all bear the title Honourable like their brothers.

STYLE OF ADDRESSING IN SPEECH

The title is never used in speech even by a servant. The eldest daughter is referred to as Miss O'Mara, the younger ones as Miss Nora and Miss Bridget O'Mara.

STYLE OF ADDRESSING IN WRITING

is the same for all. The most formal manner is:

Madam,

I have the honour to remain,
Your obedient servant,

Less formally:

Dear Madam,

Yours faithfully,

Address of envelope—
The Hon. Eileen O'Mara.

The social manner of address in writing is:

Dear Miss O'Mara,

Yours sincerely,

Address of envelope—
The Hon. Eileen O'Mara.

MARRIED DAUGHTERS OF VISCOUNTS

The daughter of a viscount, in marrying a man of lower rank than her own, keeps her title, thus:

Marriage with

A commoner	Mr Peter Green	The Hon. Mrs Green (not The Hon. Mrs. Peter Green)
A knight or baronet	Sir Bernard Brown	The Hon. Lady Brown

In marrying a man of equal or higher rank she shares her husband's title.

CHILDREN OF SONS OF VISCOUNTS
CHILDREN OF DAUGHTERS OF VISCOUNTS

have no titles or distinctions of any sort. They have, of course, a certain social precedence.

BARONS AND BARONESSES

THIS title is sometimes territorial, sometimes taken from the family name, and sometimes from other sources entirely.

The peculiar point about this title is that, unlike its foreign equivalent, it is not used in this country excepting by peeresses in their own right. In England and Wales "Baron" is, however, the legal term, whereas in Scotland the legal term for a peer of this rank is "Lord", as in Scots Law the word "Baron" denotes the property of a territorial estate held by Baronial charter.

Our example in this, the fifth and last grade of the peerage, shall be Baron Westley, with the family name of Whitworth.

STYLE OF ADDRESSING IN SPEECH

The rule of addressing all peers below ducal rank as lord and lady is equally applicable here. Baronesses in their own right, however (including women life peers), are called The Baroness————if they so wish.

STYLE OF ADDRESSING IN WRITING

The most formal manner is:

My Lord,
> I have the honour to be,
>> Your Lordship's obedient servant,

Address of envelope—
> The Right Hon. Lord Westley.

Madam,
> I have the honour to be,
>> Your Ladyship's obedient servant,

Address of envelope—
> The Right Hon. Lady Westley.

Less formally, but still not socially:

My Lord,

> Yours faithfully,

Address of envelope—
> The Right Hon. Lord Westley.

Madam,

> Yours faithfully,

Address of envelope—
> The Right Hon. Lady Westley.

The social manner of address in writing is:

Dear Lord Westley,   *or*
Dear Westley,

> Yours sincerely,

Address of envelope—
> The Lord Westley.

Dear Lady Westley,

> Yours sincerely,

Address of envelope—
> The Lady Westley.

DOWAGER BARONESSES

A dowager baroness is the earliest surviving widow of a preceding peer (but *see* p. 40 for the Scottish practice). Later surviving widows are distinguished by the use of the Christian name before the title (*see* p. 40).

STYLE OF ADDRESSING IN SPEECH

is exactly the same as if she were the reigning baroness (*see* p. 83).

STYLE OF ADDRESSING IN WRITING

The most formal manner is:

Madam,
> I have the honour to remain,
>> Your Ladyship's obedient servant,

Less formally:

Madam,
> Yours faithfully,

Address of envelope—
The Right Hon. The Dowager Lady Westley,   *or*
The Right Hon. Anne, Lady Westley.

The social manner of address in writing is:

Dear Lady Westley,
> Yours sincerely,

Address of envelope—
> The Dowager Lady Westley,   *or*
> Anne, Lady Westley.

The former wife of a Baron uses her Christian name before the title.

STYLE OF ADDRESSING IN WRITING

The most formal manner is:

Madam,
> I have the honour to remain,
>> Your Ladyship's obedient servant,

Less formally:

Madam,
> Yours faithfully,

Address of envelope—
> Anne, Lady Westley.

The social manner of address in writing is:

Dear Lady Westley,
> Yours sincerely,

Address of envelope—
> Anne, Lady Westley.

7

ELDEST SONS OF BARONS

Courtesy titles cease at the grade of an earl, so that the eldest son of a baron, like his younger brothers, is merely The Honourable, and his wife shares the title.

Example.—The Hon. Roger Whitworth.
The Hon. Mrs Whitworth.

Their visiting-cards would be inscribed Mr Whitworth and Mrs Whitworth, without the Christian name.

STYLE OF ADDRESSING IN SPEECH

As explained elsewhere, the title Honourable is never used in speech, so that the eldest son of our baron would be spoken and referred to as Mr Whitworth and his wife as Mrs Whitworth. This rule is followed by servants also.

STYLE OF ADDRESSING IN WRITING

The most formal manner is:

Sir,
I have the honour to remain,
Your obedient servant,

Less formally:

Dear Sir,
Yours faithfully,

Address of envelope—
The Hon. Roger Whitworth.

Madam,
I have the honour to remain,
Your obedient servant,

Less formally:

Dear Madam,
Yours faithfully,

Address of envelope—
The Hon. Mrs Whitworth.

The social manner of address in writing is:

Dear Mr Whitworth,   *or*
Dear Whitworth,
                        Yours sincerely,

  Address of envelope—
                    The Hon. Roger Whitworth.

Dear Mrs Whitworth,
                        Yours sincerely,

  Address of envelope—
                    The Hon. Mrs Whitworth.

WIDOWS OF ELDEST SONS OF BARONS

keep their title until re-marriage, when it is abandoned in favour of the second husband's status, whether it be higher or lower. This does not apply, of course, if the widow possesses a title in her own right. The same rules apply to former wives as to widows, except that it is usual for a former wife to insert her own Christian name, e.g.
                    The Hon. Mrs Diana Whitworth.

ELDEST SONS OF SCOTTISH BARONS (LORDS)

In the case of peerages created before the Union (1707) the eldest sons (indeed legally the *nearest heir*, even if grandson, brother, uncle or nephew) are called The Master of ———. Their wives are called The Hon. Mrs ———, without the husband's Christian name.

              Example.—The Master of Ballantrae.
                    The Hon. Mrs Scott of Ballantrae.

STYLE OF ADDRESSING IN SPEECH

Formerly styled "My Lord", he is nowadays called Sir on formal occasions, and socially he is called by his surname, Mr Scott (or more familiarly Scott). In the household and family he is referred to as The Master, and servants address him as Master. His wife, like her English counterpart, is called Mrs Scott.

STYLE OF ADDRESSING IN WRITING

The formal manner is:

Sir (or Dear Sir),

Address of envelope—
> The Master of Ballantrae.

Madam,

Address of envelope—
> The Hon. Mrs Scott of Ballantrae.

The social manner of address in writing is:

Dear Mr Scott,   *or*
Dear Scott,

Address of envelope—
> The Master of Ballantrae.

Dear Mrs Scott,

Address of envelope—
> The Hon. Mrs Scott of Ballantrae.

In the case of Scottish baronies created since the Union the English form of address is used (*see* p. 83).

YOUNGER SONS OF BARONS
WIVES OF YOUNGER SONS OF BARONS
WIDOWS OF YOUNGER SONS OF BARONS
FORMER WIVES OF YOUNGER SONS OF
    BARONS

The same rules exactly apply here as to younger sons of earls and their wives (*see* pp. 72 and 73).

DAUGHTERS OF BARONS

all bear the title Honourable, and the same rules apply as for daughters of viscounts (*see* p. 81).

MARRIED DAUGHTERS OF BARONS

The daughter of a baron, in marrying a man of lower rank than her own, keeps her title, thus:

Marriage with

A commoner	Mr Peter Green	The Hon. Mrs Green (not The Hon. Mrs. Peter Green)
A knight or baronet	Sir Bernard Brown	The Hon. Lady Brown

In marrying a man of equal or higher rank she shares her husband's title.

CHILDREN OF SONS OF BARONS
CHILDREN OF DAUGHTERS OF BARONS

have no titles or distinctions of any sort.

MALTESE NOBILITY

are known as "Holders of Titles recognized by the Crown" and are addressed The Most Noble.

BARONETS

THIS title, identified by the prefix Sir to Christian and surname, is a hereditary honour descending from father to son. Failing a son to the first holder, the title becomes extinct; but failing a son to a later holder, the title goes to the nearest male descendant of a former holder. It is distinguished from that of knight by the word baronet, or one of its contractions, being added at the end of the name, thus:

Sir George Robinson, Bt.

Where a Scottish family uses a territorial title this is inserted before the addition "Bt.".

Sir George Robinson of Glenrobinson, Bt.

The word baronet is used in full only in formal documents. Bt. is the older abbreviation and the only one recognized by the Council of the Baronetage, but, in spite of this, Bart. is still much used. This is a pity, because it is considered wrong by those who know and prefer the right way.

A baronet's wife takes the title of Lady in conjunction with the surname only—never with her own or her husband's Christian name unless she happens to have a title of her own (*see* pp. 45, 54, 64, 74, 81 and 89).

Example.—Lady Robinson.

She is not entitled to be called The Lady Robinson (*see* p. 45).

The only exception to this rule might be the written one of Lady (George) Robinson, when it is necessary to distinguish her from another Lady Robinson. In actual speech there can be no such distinction. In Scotland, however, the territorial addition (if it exists) acts as the distinction:

> Lady Robinson of Glenrobinson.

STYLE OF ADDRESSING IN SPEECH

A baronet is addressed by his title and Christian name, as, for instance, Sir George, and spoken of as Sir George Robinson, or, more familiarly, as Sir George. There is no distinction here between a baronet and a knight.

STYLE OF ADDRESSING IN WRITING

The most formal manner is:

Sir,

> I have the honour to remain,
> > Your obedient servant,

Less formally, but still not socially:

Dear Sir,

> Yours faithfully,

Address of envelope—
> Sir George Robinson, Bt.
> Sir George Robinson of Glenrobinson, Bt.

Madam,

> I have the honour to remain,
> > Your Ladyship's obedient servant,

Less formally, but still not socially:

Dear Madam,

> Yours faithfully,

Address of envelope—
> Lady Robinson.
> Lady Robinson of Glenrobinson.

The social manner of address in writing is:

Dear Sir George Robinson,
                    Yours sincerely,

                or more familiarly

Dear Sir George,   *or*
Dear Robinson,
                    Yours sincerely,

  Address of envelope—
                    Sir George Robinson, Bt.

Dear Lady Robinson,
                    Yours sincerely,

  Address of envelope—
                    Lady Robinson.

BARONETESS

There are very few baronetcies (all of them are Scottish) where it is possible for a lady to inherit the title. Only one is at present held by a lady. She is addressed in the same way as a baronet's wife; but where for a baronet the abbreviation Bt. would be added, her name should be followed by Btss.

  Address of envelope—
        Lady Robinson of Glenrobinson, Btss.

WIDOWS OF BARONETS

retain their style of address unless and until the succeeding baronet marries, when the widow is called either

            The Dowager Lady Robinson,   *or*
            Dora, Lady Robinson.

The rule follows that of the peerage (*see* p. 40).

STYLE OF ADDRESSING IN SPEECH

is the same as for a baronet's wife (*see* p. 90).

STYLE OF ADDRESSING IN WRITING

The most formal manner is:

Madam,
> I have the honour to remain,
> > Your Ladyship's obedient servant,

Less formally:

Dear Madam,
> Yours faithfully,

Address of envelope—
> The Dowager Lady Robinson,   *or*
> Dora, Lady Robinson.

The social manner of address in writing is:

Dear Lady Robinson,
> Yours sincerely,

Address of envelope—
> The Dowager Lady Robinson,   *or*
> Dora, Lady Robinson.

WIDOWS OF BARONETS RE-MARRYING

If marrying a peer, an honourable, or another baronet, the title and name of the new husband is taken. If she marries an untitled gentleman, she becomes Mrs ————.

FORMER WIVES OF BARONETS

Until remarriage they are addressed in the same way as widows, except that they will not be Dowager, but will use a Christian name before the title.

CHILDREN OF BARONETS

have no titles or distinctions, excepting that the eldest son's Christian name is not used.

Example.—Mr Robinson.

In Scottish families which have a territorial designation (*see* p. 105), he is styled "younger" (which may be abbreviated yr.) of the family description.

Example.—Mr Robinson, younger of Glenrobinson.

HONOURABLES

When the son of a viscount or baron, or the younger son of an earl, receives a baronetcy, the foregoing rules apply, excepting as to the address of envelopes, which should be:

The Hon. Sir George Robinson, Bt.
The Hon. Lady Robinson.

KNIGHTS

THE orders of knighthood are various, but not one of them is hereditary. We will take them in the order of their precedence and deal with general rules as they arise.

THE MOST NOBLE ORDER OF THE GARTER

This order is conferred most often, but not exclusively, upon royalties and in the peerage. It is distinguished by the letters K.G. after the name and title:

> *Example.*—The Duke of Middlesex, K.G.

THE MOST ANCIENT AND MOST NOBLE ORDER OF THE THISTLE

This order is conferred exclusively upon Scottish nobles (these include both peers and certain commoners as nobles in the technical sense) and is distinguished by the letters K.T. after the name and title.

> *Example.*—The Earl of Queensferry, K.T.
> Sir William MacHector of Drimmore, K.T.

THE MOST ILLUSTRIOUS ORDER OF ST. PATRICK

This order was conferred exclusively upon Irish nobles, and distinguished by the letters K.P. after the name and title.

> *Example.*—The Viscount O'Mara, K.P.

No appointments have been made to the order since 1922.

THE MOST HONOURABLE ORDER OF THE BATH

This is the first of the orders of knighthood in which there is more than one class. Women as well as men are eligible. Members of the first two classes only are knights, and the use of the title in speech and writing is the same as for baronets and their wives and children (excepting, of course, the abbreviation Bt.).

The classes and distinctions, for men, are as follows:

Knights Grand Cross	.	Sir Robert Johnson, G.C.B.
Knights Commanders	.	Sir Edward Thompson, K.C.B.
Companions	. .	Richard Jackson, Esq., C.B.

The wives of companions, as such, have no distinctions, though they have recognized precedence. The classes for women are:

Dames Grand Cross	.	Dame Matilda Johnson, G.C.B.
Dames Commanders	.	Dame Pamela Thompson, D.C.B.
Companions	. .	Mrs Jackson, C.B.

Husbands of ladies raised to any one of the ranks in this order do not share their wives' distinctions.

The title carried by the first two degrees of this order is used always in conjunction with the lady's Christian name. The formal mode of address in speech is "Dame Matilda" or "Dame Pamela". The most formal address in writing is:

Madam,

I beg to remain,

Your obedient servant,

Less formally:

Dear Madam,

Yours faithfully,

The social manner of address in writing is:

Dear Dame Matilda Johnson, *or*
Dear Dame Matilda,

> Yours sincerely,

Address of envelope—
> Dame Matilda Johnson, G.C.B. (or D.C.B.).

Where the recipient of this honour already enjoys a higher title, either by birth or marriage, the accepted rule would seem to be that for a peeress, or the daughter of a duke, marquess, or earl, her title in this order is indicated only by the letters following her name; that the prefix "The Hon." should be used with and preceding "Dame" (as with a knight); and that the wives or widows of baronets and knights may themselves choose whether they wish to be known as, e.g., Lady Jones, D.C.B., or Dame Bronwen Jones, D.C.B.

THE MOST EXALTED ORDER OF THE STAR OF INDIA

As in the previous case, this order (which is no longer conferred) has three classes. Members of the first two classes only are knights, and the use of the title in speech and writing is the same as for baronets and their wives and children (excepting, of course, the abbreviation Bt.).

Knights Grand Commanders	Sir Robert Johnson, G.C.S.I.
Knights Commanders .	Sir Edward Thompson, K.C.S.I.
Companions . .	Richard Jackson, Esq., C.S.I.

The wives of companions, as such, have no distinctions, though they have recognized precedence.

THE MOST DISTINGUISHED ORDER OF ST. MICHAEL AND ST. GEORGE

There are three classes in this order, for which women as well as men are eligible:

Knights Grand Cross	.	Sir Robert Johnson, G.C.M.G.
Knights Commanders	.	Sir Edward Thompson, K.C.M.G.
Companions	. .	Richard Jackson, Esq., C.M.G.

Members of the first two classes only are knights, and the use of the title in speech and writing is the same as for baronets and their wives and children (excepting, of course, the abbreviation Bt.). The wives of companions, as such, have no distinctions, though they have recognized precedence.

The three classes for women are:

Dames Grand Cross	.	Dame Matilda Johnson, G.C.M.G.
Dames Commanders	.	Dame Pamela Thompson, D.C.M.G.
Companions	. .	Mrs Jackson, C.M.G.

Husbands of ladies raised to any one of the ranks in this order do not share their wives' distinctions.

The title carried by the first two degrees of this order is used always in conjunction with the lady's Christian name. The formal mode of address in speech is "Dame Matilda" or "Dame Pamela". The most formal mode of address in writing is:

Madam,

I beg to remain,

Your obedient servant,

Less formally:

Dear Madam,

Yours faithfully,

The social manner of address in writing is:

Dear Dame Matilda Johnson, *or* Dear Dame Matilda,
Yours sincerely,

Address of envelope—
Dame Matilda Johnson, G.C.M.G. (or D.C.M.G.)

The use of the title carried by the first two degrees of this order (except, of course, that the letters after the name are G.C.M.G. or D.C.M.G.) is the same as for the Order of the Bath (*see* p. 96).

THE MOST EMINENT ORDER OF THE INDIAN EMPIRE

There are three classes in this order (which is no longer conferred), members of the first two classes only being knights. The use of the title in speech and writing is the same as for baronets and their wives and children (excepting, of course, the abbreviation Bt.). The wives of companions, as such, have no distinctions, though they have recognized precedence.

Knights Grand
              Commanders   Sir Robert Johnson, G.C.I.E.
Knights Commanders .   Sir Edward Thompson, K.C.I.E.
Companions   .   .   Richard Jackson, Esq., C.I.E.

THE ROYAL VICTORIAN ORDER

There are five classes in this order, for which women as well as men are eligible:

Knights Grand Cross .   Sir Robert Johnson, G.C.V.O.
Knights Commanders .   Sir Edward Thompson, K.C.V.O.
Commanders   .   .   Richard Jackson, Esq., C.V.O.
Members Fourth Class .   Herbert Black, Esq., M.V.O.
Members Fifth Class .   Charles White, Esq., M.V.O.

Members of the first two classes only are knights, and the use of the title in speech and writing (excepting, of course, the abbreviation Bt.) is the same as for baronets and their wives and children. The wives of commanders and members, as such, have no distinctions, though they have recognized precedence.

The five classes for women are:

Dames Grand Cross .	Dame Matilda Johnson, G.C.V.O.
Dames Commanders .	Dame Pamela Thompson, D.C.V.O.
Commanders . . .	Mrs Jackson, C.V.O.
Members Fourth Class	Mrs Black, M.V.O.
Members Fifth Class .	Miss Brown, M.V.O.

Husbands of ladies raised to any one of the ranks in this order do not share their wives' distinctions.

The use of the title carried by the first two degrees of this order (except, of course, that the letters after the name are G.C.V.O. or D.C.V.O.) is the same as for the Order of the Bath (*see* p. 96).

THE MOST EXCELLENT ORDER OF THE BRITISH EMPIRE

This order is the most recent, and women as well as men are eligible. The five classes for men are:

Knights Grand Cross .	Sir Robert Johnson, G.B.E.
Knights Commanders .	Sir Edward Thompson, K.B.E.
Commanders . .	Richard Jackson, Esq., C.B.E.
Officers . . .	Herbert Black, Esq., O.B.E.
Members . . .	Thomas Brown, Esq., M.B.E.

Members of the first two classes only are knights, and the use of the title in speech and writing (except, of course, the abbreviation Bt.) is the same as for baronets and their wives and children. The wives of commanders, officers, and members, as such, have no distinctions, though they have recognized precedence.

The five classes for women are:

Dames Grand Cross	.	Dame Matilda Johnson, G.B.E.
Dames Commanders	.	Dame Pamela Thompson, D.B.E.
Commanders	. .	Mrs Jackson, C.B.E.
Officers	. . .	Mrs Black, O.B.E.
Members	. . .	Miss Brown, M.B.E.

Husbands of ladies raised to any one of the ranks in this order do not share their wives' distinctions.

The use of the title carried by the first two degrees of this order (except, of course, that the letters after the name are G.B.E. or D.B.E.) is the same as for the Order of the Bath (*see* p. 96).

KNIGHTS BACHELOR

This is the lowest order of knighthood, and is designated thus:

Sir William Jones,

that is, with Christian name (not initials) and surname preceded by the title Sir.

Only in formal documents is the word Knight or the abbreviation Kt. sometimes added to the name. It is never correct to use the letters K.B. to signify a Knight Bachelor. In all other respects the use of the title in speech and writing (except, of course, the abbreviation Bt.) is the same as for baronets and their wives and children (*see* pp. 90 to 94).

WIDOWS OF KNIGHTS
WIDOWS OF KNIGHTS RE-MARRYING

See under BARONETS (pp. 92 and 93).

HONORARY ORDERS OF KNIGHTHOOD

These are conferred from time to time on foreigners. Except in rare cases granted specially by the Sovereign, the recipient has no right to the title of Sir and it should not be used before the name; but the letters signifying membership of an order may be used after the name, without the abbreviation Hon., e.g.

Mr Albert C. Gould, K.B.E.

NEW TITLES (KNIGHTS AND DAMES)

All persons awarded Orders, decorations, and medals may add the appropriate letters to their names immediately after the announcement in the *London Gazette*, e.g.:

John Smith, Esq., C.B.E.
Major Evan Jones, M.C.
Corporal William Brown, M.M.

Knights Grand Cross and Knights Commanders of Orders of Chivalry and Knights Bachelor may use the prefix "Sir" immediately after the official announcement in the *London Gazette*.

A Knight's appointment is completed when he receives the accolade from the Sovereign. In very rare cases, where personal investiture is impracticable, Letters Patent granting full privileges of the honour are issued.

Ladies who are appointed Dames Grand Cross or Dames Commanders of Orders of Chivalry can assume the prefix "Dame" as soon as the notice appears in the *London Gazette*.

GENERAL REMARKS

All the letters signifying membership of orders, and all decorations, should be used in addressing, subject to the point made below, that a lower rank in an order is absorbed in a higher. These letters are shown in the correct order on p. 169.

In the case of a Knight Bachelor being also a companion in another order, his designation would be:

Sir Henry Jones, C.B.

In this case the letters K.C.B. would be wrong, because, although a knight and a member of the Order of the Bath, he is not a knight in that particular order.

When a member of an order of knighthood is promoted to a higher rank within the same order, the lower rank is absorbed in the higher and therefore the designation of the lower rank is omitted after the name. Thus when Richard Jackson, Esq., C.V.O., is created a knight of the Royal Victorian Order he becomes Sir Richard Jackson, K.C.V.O.

When the son of a viscount or baron or the younger son of an earl receives a knighthood, the foregoing rules apply, excepting as to the address of envelopes, which should be:

The Hon. Sir William Browning, K.C.M.G. (or otherwise).
The Hon. Lady Browning.

CHIEFS OF SCOTTISH CLANS
AND TERRITORIAL HOUSES (LAIRDS)

By Scots Law, and ancient custom, to which they rightly cling, Chiefs of Scottish Clans and Names, chieftains, and lairds are known by chiefly styles or territorial designations which are legally part of their surnames. Mr is not used, and Esq. seldom. Mackvicular of Mackvicular is called Mackvicular in his own territorial district or gathering, and elsewhere The Mackvicular—if he be chief of a *whole* "Name" or "clan" (The Armstrength, and The Mackvicular, are not translations of the Gaelic *An*, but a 15th-century Scots style). MacHector of Drimmore is called Drimmore.

The style of address in speech is Mackvicular, or Drimmore, *without* Mr—whatever the rank of the speaker.

The normal mode of address in writing is Sir (or Dear Sir)—but a clansman would write Dear Chief.

The social mode of address is:

> Dear Mackvicular, *or* Dear Drimmore.

The address of envelopes has varied and may be:

> John Mackvicular of Mackvicular, Esq., *or*
> James MacHector of Drimmore, Esq.,

but since most chiefs were feudal Barons (who had precedence of ordinary Esquires), the tendency is, again, to omit both Christian name and Esq.; thus:

> The Mackvicular of Mackvicular, *or*
> MacHector of Drimmore.

Any decorations follow the territorial designation.

Their wives are addressed formally in writing as:

Madam (or Dear Madam),

and socially as:

> Dear Mrs Mackvicular of Mackvicular,   *or*
> Dear Mrs MacHector of Drimmore,

They are introduced or announced as:

> Mrs Mackvicular of Mackvicular,   *or*
> Mrs MacHector of Drimmore.

Their heirs are addressed in writing as:

> John Mackvicular, younger of Mackvicular,   *or*
> James MacHector, younger of Drimmore,

and they are also introduced or announced in this way. All unmarried daughters use the title, thus:

> Miss MacHector of Drimmore—for the eldest, and
> Miss Jean MacHector of Drimmore—for a younger one.

It is not the custom for younger sons to use the title.

The old Scottish title of "Laird" is still freely used in Scotland, and even a landless chief can be styled in writing, or referred to in speech, as The Laird of Mackvicular, and any other proprietor is styled, e.g. The Laird of Drimmore.

Their wives are in rural Scotland still styled (and legally so, if the wife of a chief, or feudal baron) as:

> The Lady Mackvicular,   *or*   The Lady Drimmore.

Southern Society deprecated (whilst local custom retained) these titles, and "Mrs" (which has a different origin) was introduced from England towards the close of the 18th century. Technically the "Madam" retained by wives of Irish Chieftains is correct, and a few Scottish ones now use it.

The widow of a Chief or Laird continues to use the territorial style and the prefix Dowager is used in the same circumstances as where it is applied to a Peeress (*see* p. 40):

> The Dowager Mrs Mackvicular of Mackvicular.

IRISH CHIEFTAINS

UNDER the Brehon Law, the succession of Irish chieftains was by selection within a limited family group (*deirbhfine*), but the principle of seniority was observed by Gaelic genealogists. About the beginning of the 19th century some of the representatives of the last holders of the chieftainries resumed the appropriate designations, which had lapsed with the destruction of the Gaelic order.

The descent of the following by primogeniture in the male line from the last inaugurated or *de facto* chieftain has been examined by the Genealogical Office, Dublin Castle. Subject to the possible survival in some cases of senior lines at present unidentified, they are recorded at the Genealogical Office as Chiefs of the Name and are recognized by courtesy. Certain chiefs whose pedigrees have not been finally proved are included in this list on account of their prescriptive standing.

Mac Dermot Prince of Coolavin.

Mac Gillycuddy of the Reeks.

Mac Murrough Kavanagh.

O Brien of Thomond.

O Callaghan.

O Conor Don.

O Donel of Tirconnell.

O Donoghue of the Glens.

O Donovan.

O Morchoe.

O Neill of Clandeboy.

O Sionnaigh (called The Fox since 1552).

O Toole of Fer Tire.

O Grady of Kilballyowen.

O Kelly of Gallagh and Tycooly.

The address on the envelope is as the above designation (e.g. O Donoghue of the Glens), or with the prefix "The", which although not officially recognized is generally used (e.g. The Mac Dermot). The social mode of address is "Dear O Donoghue", etc.

There are three knights of a palatine creation by an Earl of Desmond in the 14th century, the Knight of Glin, the Knight of Kerry, and the White Knight (this last title is dormant). They are so designated, and so addressed on the envelope.

The social mode of address is "Dear Knight of Glin", etc.

The wives of persons designated chieftains are addressed as "Madam O Donoghue", etc. The wives of the knights palatine are addressed as the wives of chieftains (but the Knight of Kerry is a baronet, and his wife should be addressed as a baronet's wife).

The sons and daughters are addressed as the children of an Esquire.

ESQUIRES

THE use of this title for every man who cannot claim a higher one persists, far more widely than used to be the case, when social usage limited its application to those considered to merit it through social standing, membership of one of the professions, possession of a degree from Oxford or Cambridge University, and so on. It is felt to be more courteous in general to use it in all correspondence, although a reaction, influenced by usage in the United States and some other English-speaking countries, now leads many writers, especially in business, to prefer the use of Mr. Whichever style is preferred, it should clearly be used consistently, since the difficulty of ascertaining which of one's correspondents is *entitled* to the appellation Esquire must rule out any thought of using it only where it was, in the past, conferred by social position or other qualification. It should, however, not be used in addressing Quakers, who dislike the form.

The title Esquire should never be used in conjunction with any other title, as for instance the prefix Mr. Some doubt arises occasionally as to the lesser grades of orders of knighthood. Commanders, Companions, Officers and Members of the various orders of knighthood are addressed as esquires with the distinguishing abbreviation after the name, thus:

Richard Jackson, Esq., C.V.O.

(For fuller details *see under* KNIGHTS, p. 95).

This being so, the following are the correct uses for the head of the family. The formal manner of address in speech is Sir, and the social manner Mr Robins. His wife

is called Madam, and referred to as Mrs Robins. The most
formal manner of address in writing is:

Sir,

> I beg to remain, Sir,
>> Your obedient servant,

Madam,

> I beg to remain, Madam,
>> Your obedient servant,

Less formally, but still not socially:

Dear Sir,

> Yours faithfully,

Dear Madam,

> Yours faithfully,

The social manner of address in writing is:

Dear Mr Robins,

> Yours sincerely,

Dear Mrs Robins,

> Yours sincerely,

Address of envelopes—
Harold Robins, Esq., or H. J. Robins, Esq.,
Mrs. Robins, Mrs. Harold Robins, or Mrs. H. J. Robins.

(If the person concerned has two or more forenames, it
is preferable to use initials; if one only, the name in full.)

For all other male members of the family the rules are
the same, but envelopes to their wives always include
their husbands' Christian names, for instance:

Mrs John Robins.

Wives of commoners take precedence in the family
from their husbands, as in the titled classes. Once a
woman marries the head of the family, or the man who
subsequently becomes the head of the family, this position

remains with her for life, unless she re-marries or the marriage is dissolved.

It is wrong to change the form of address on widowhood; Mrs John Robins remains Mrs John Robins when her husband dies, and should not be addressed by her own Christian name. This error might moreover lead strangers to suppose that her marriage had been dissolved; a former wife would normally use her own Christian name or initials, thus:

> Mrs Mary Robins.
> Mrs M. A. Robins.

SONS

bearing the same name or initials as their fathers may be addressed:

> Harold Robins, Jnr., Esq.,

if this is necessary to avoid confusion.

There was a Victorian habit of addressing young men of nursery and school age as Master Robins, which seems happily to have died out. Now the more sensible manner of addressing all boys is simply Harold Robins, until they are grown up and worthy of the title Esq.

DAUGHTERS

The eldest unmarried daughter of the head of the family is Miss Robins. All other unmarried women in the family use their distinguishing Christian names, for example:

> Miss Jane Robins.

DOUBLE NAMES

THE justification for a hyphenated double name is when two land-owning families have been merged into one through marriage, or when legal licence to adopt it has been obtained. The form need not be denied, however, to those who use a second Christian name prefixed to the surname for distinction or for convenience, though in such cases a hyphen should not be used. In speech as well as writing the two names are always used.

PRESIDENTS OF SOCIETIES

are addressed in formal speech and writing as Sir or Mr President. In the case of a titled holder of the office he would be addressed according to his rank, e.g. My Lord Duke (or Your Grace) and President, or My Lord and President, etc. Where a woman holds office she is addressed as Madam President (except that a duchess would be Your Grace and President). In all cases envelopes are addressed according to name and rank, with the addition of

President of The ————.

PRIVY COUNSELLORS

THIS office is conferred for life, but it is not hereditary. All members of the Cabinet must be privy counsellors, but all privy counsellors are not members of the Cabinet. Women as well as men may be appointed privy counsellors.

There is nothing to indicate this rank in the style of addressing in speech, which is according to the holder's rank otherwise, but in writing the name is preceded with the distinction The Right Hon. Wives do not share this title. In the case of the peerage the office of privy counsellor is not indicated, as in the three lowest grades the title of Right Hon. is already used and in the two highest grades it is assumed to be incorporated in the loftier titles (*see* p. 45).

Examples are as follows: A commoner is referred and spoken to as Mr Williams, while the manner of address in writing is, formally,

Sir (or Dear Sir),

I have the honour to be, Sir (or Dear Sir),
Yours faithfully,

less formally,

Dear Sir,

Yours faithfully,

or socially

Dear Mr Williams,

Yours sincerely,

Address of envelope in all cases—

The Right Hon. James Williams.
Esq. is not used.

His wife does not share the title, and would therefore always be addressed in speech and writing as Mrs Williams.

A lady who is appointed privy counsellor is referred and spoken to as Mrs Matilda Johnson, while the formal manner of address in writing is: The Right Hon. Matilda Johnson, omitting Mrs or Miss. Husbands of ladies appointed privy counsellors do not share this title.

In the case of Navy, Army or Air Force officers the style of address in writing is, for example,

Admiral The Right Hon. Sir James Smith

or

Colonel The Right Hon. Henry Jones

or

Air Vice-Marshal The Right Hon. Sir Josiah Blank.

In the case of Church dignitaries the style of address in writing would be, for example,

The Most Revd. and Right Hon. The Lord Archbishop of Blank.

The Right Revd. and Right Hon. The Lord Bishop of Blank.

CHAIRMAN OF THE GREATER LONDON COUNCIL

Rules as for privy counsellors apply (*see* p. 112), excepting that the prefix Right Hon. ceases on retirement.

Address of envelope—
The Right Hon. The Chairman of the Greater London Council, *or*
The Right Hon. James Brown, but, on retirement,
James Brown, Esq.

ECCLESIASTICAL

THE CHURCH OF ENGLAND
Lords Spiritual

The Archbishops of Canterbury and York, the Bishops of London, Durham, and Winchester, and twenty-one of the other English Diocesan Bishops in order of seniority constitute the Lords Spiritual in Parliament. The Bishop of Sodor and Man is not summoned.

Archbishops

The Archbishop of Canterbury ranks next in precedence to the Royal Family, and above dukes in the Roll of Peerage. The Archbishop of York ranks next to the Lord Chancellor.

Style of Addressing in Speech

The manner of addressing the Archbishops of Canterbury and York in speech both by equals and inferiors is "Your Grace". They are referred to by their territorial titles, e.g. The Archbishop of Canterbury, and not by name; but where no confusion is likely, "the Archbishop" is sufficient. Only past or retired prelates are referred to by name, e.g. Archbishop Temple.

Style of Addressing in Writing

The most formal manner is:

My Lord Archbishop, *or*
Your Grace,

> I have the honour to remain, my Lord Archbishop,
> > Your Grace's devoted and obedient servant,

Less formally:

My Lord Archbishop,
> Yours faithfully,

The Archbishops of Canterbury and York, being privy counsellors, are addressed on the envelope as:

> The Most Revd. and Right Hon. The Lord Archbishop of Canterbury (or York).

Other Archbishops are addressed on the envelope, both formally and socially, as:

> The Most Revd. The Lord Archbishop of —.

The social manner of address in writing is:

Dear Lord Archbishop,   *or*
Dear Archbishop,

Yours sincerely,

The same modes of address are applicable to all Archbishops of the Anglican Communion in accordance with the general principles set out below (*see* BISHOPS, p. 117). An exception, however, occurs in the case of the Archbishop of Armagh, who is addressed thus:

The Most Revd. His Grace The Lord Primate of all Ireland.

SIGNATURES

A reigning archbishop uses his Christian name in English or Latin, or the initials of his Christian names, coupled with the Latin name of his see, or some abbreviation of it (when the abbreviated Latin name of the see is used it is usual to put a colon instead of a full stop). The Archbishop of Canterbury signs himself Michael Cantuar:, and the Archbishop of York signs Donald Ebor:.

WIVES OF ARCHBISHOPS

The wife of an archbishop does not share her husband's precedence unless, of course, he possesses a temporal title as well as the spiritual one, in which case rules previously given would apply. Otherwise she is plain Mrs.

RETIRED ARCHBISHOPS

On resigning, an archbishop, though relinquishing his legal, constitutional, and ecclesiastical status as archbishop, remains a bishop. By courtesy nevertheless he is still addressed as archbishop, unless having perhaps held archiepiscopal office overseas, he should be appointed a bishop in this country, when he will be so addressed. This will be so if the appointment be as diocesan, suffragan or assistant bishop, according to the rule for each.

Upon the retirement of Lord Davidson of Lambeth from the Archbishopric of Canterbury a temporal title was bestowed upon the retiring Primate, who otherwise would also have renounced his seat in the House of Lords. This course was followed also in the cases of Archbishops Lang and Fisher. The most formal manner of address in such cases is:

My Lord,   *or*
My Lord Archbishop,

> I have the honour to remain, my Lord (or My Lord Archbishop),
>
> > Your devoted and obedient servant,

Address of envelope—
> The Most Revd. The Lord Davidson of Lambeth.

In all other cases the formal manner of address is in polite usage the same, except for the mode of address on the envelope which should be:

Address of envelope—
> > The Most Revd. John Brown.

Retired Archbishops are addressed and referred to in speech, both socially and formally, by title and surname.

Example.—Archbishop Brown, *or* Archbishop Lord Lang.

They use their ordinary signatures, with the addition of Archbishop or Bishop.

BISHOPS

It is common knowledge that the title "Lord Bishop" is not confined to those English diocesan bishops who happen by reason of seniority to have seats in the House of Lords. All diocesan bishops of England are described in legal documents as Lord Bishops. Nor can the title be traced to the fact that bishops were formerly barons also, possessing land and revenues accordingly. The title *Dominus Episcopus* was in use before the Conquest and before the bishops were constituted barons.

All the bishops of the Anglican Communion have come by custom or right to be styled Lord Bishops. The title owes nothing to special grant or to any act of sovereignty by monarch. From time immemorial the Episcopal character and office have attracted forms of address of highest dignity and reverence. Their variable forms have taken their present shape of Lord Bishop, a title which may be used with propriety of all episcopally consecrated bishops. Though in the Eastern churches titles more splendid and picturesque are in use, Lord Bishop is never wrong.

Among bishops of the Anglican Communion there are some in Missionary sees who modestly discourage the use of the title. Until lately it has been unknown in the American Episcopal Church, so far as domestic use is concerned, but American bishops should in courtesy be addressed by English-speaking correspondents outside the U.S.A. in the manner applicable to all other bishops of the Anglican Communion. The American style "Right Reverend Sir" is, indeed, giving place occasionally to "My Lord" in U.S.A.

The twenty-four English bishops who, with the two

archbishops, have seats in the House of Lords, rank below viscounts and above barons. The manner of address in speech is My Lord and His Lordship, both formally and socially.

The most formal manner of address in writing is:

My Lord, *or*
My Lord Bishop,
                    I have the honour to remain,
                              Your Lordship's obedient servant,
    Less formally, but still not socially:
My Lord,
                              Yours faithfully,
    The social manner of address is:
Dear Lord Bishop, *or* Dear Bishop,
                              Yours sincerely,
    Address of envelope in all cases—
        The Right Revd. The Lord Bishop of ————.

BISHOPS SUFFRAGAN

In the United Kingdom they are not addressed as such but by courtesy exactly as diocesan bishops; they are styled Bishop of ————, not Bishop Suffragan of whatever the diocese may be. (The Bishops Suffragan of Grantham and Grimsby are addressed as though they were diocesan bishops of sees of these names, and not as Bishops Suffragan in the diocese of Lincoln.) In Canada and Australia, however, although they may (particularly in Canada) be given a territorial style of their own, they are thought of and addressed as suffragans of the diocese:

        The Right Revd. The Suffragan Bishop of ————.

BISHOPS OF THE ANGLICAN COMMUNION

The manner of address in speech and writing, both formally and socially, is exactly the same as for English bishops. There are, however, the following minor points of distinction to be borne in mind.

IRISH BISHOPS

The manner of address in speech and writing is the same as for English bishops.

The exception is the Bishop of Meath, who is addressed as "The Most Revd." instead of "The Right Revd.", as Premier Bishop of the Church of Ireland.

SCOTTISH BISHOPS

The same as for Irish bishops (*see above*). The Primus is addressed in speech and writing as "My Lord" or "My Lord Primus".

Address of envelope—
The Most Revd. The Primus.

BISHOPS COADJUTOR

In the Anglican church overseas Bishops Coadjutor may be appointed to assist an Archbishop. They have no separate territorial style, and are addressed by name, with the addition of their office:

The Right Revd. A. B. ————,
Bishop Coadjutor of ————.

ASSISTANT BISHOPS

In Britain Assistant Bishops may be appointed, after retirement as a diocesan or suffragan, to assist the bishop of the diocese in which they are living. They are addressed by name. In the Anglican church overseas this title may be given to younger men who after consecration are appointed to assist the bishop of a large diocese. The form of address is the same in either case:

The Right Revd. C. D. ————.

RETIRED BISHOPS

Retired bishops are addressed by their names, but otherwise as for English bishops:

Example.—Dear Lord Bishop, *or* Dear Bishop, *and envelopes should be addressed—*
> The Right Revd. John Brown.

WIVES OF BISHOPS (Rules as for ARCHBISHOPS, p. 115).

DEANS

are addressed in speech as Mr Dean or Dean. The most formal manner of address in writing is:

Very Reverend Sir,
> I have the honour to remain, Very Reverend Sir,
>> Your obedient servant,

Less formally, but not socially or on a church matter:

Dear Sir,
> Yours faithfully,

The social manner of address in writing is:

Dear Mr Dean, *or*
Dear Dean,
> Yours sincerely,

Address of envelope—
> The Very Revd. The Dean of ————.

Deans who are also Bishops are addressed as The Right Revd. The Dean of ————.

RETIRED DEANS

have no right to the title on retirement, and are addressed as other members of the clergy (*see* p. 123), but if the title Dean Emeritus is conferred they are addressed as deans (also, by courtesy, if it is known that they wish to retain the title), except that the envelope would be addressed in the personal name, thus:

The Very Revd. Charles Cox, D.D.

PROVOSTS

are the incumbents of those parish churches which have become cathedrals in recent times. They take rank and precedence as deans and are addressed in speech as Mr Provost. The most formal manner of address in writing is:

Very Reverend Sir,
I have the honour to remain, Very Reverend Sir,
Your obedient servant,

Less formally, but not socially or on a church matter:

Dear Sir,
Yours faithfully,

The social manner of address in writing is:

Dear Mr Provost,　*or*
Dear Provost,
Yours sincerely,

Address of envelope in both cases—
The Very Revd. The Provost of ————.

RETIRED PROVOSTS.　Rules as for retired deans apply.

ARCHDEACONS

are addressed in speech as Mr Archdeacon. The most formal manner of address in writing is:

Venerable Sir,
I have the honour to remain, Venerable Sir,
Your obedient servant,

Less formally, but not socially or on a church matter:
Dear Sir,

> Yours faithfully,

The social manner of address in writing is:

Dear Mr Archdeacon,   *or*
Dear Archdeacon,

> Yours sincerely,

Address of envelope in both cases—
> The Venerable The Archdeacon of ————.

Retired Archdeacons

have no right to the title on retirement, and are addressed as other members of the clergy (*see* p. 123), but if the title Archdeacon Emeritus is conferred on them (also, by courtesy, if it is known that they wish to retain the title), they are addressed in speech as Mr Archdeacon and referred to as Archdeacon ———— (using surname), except in official documents.

Address of envelope—
> The Venerable Arthur Holt, D.D.

Canons

are either residentiary or honorary. The rule is the same in each case. They are addressed in speech as Canon ————. The most formal manner of address in writing is:

Reverend Sir,

> I have the honour to remain, Reverend Sir,
> Your obedient servant,

Less formally, but not socially or on a church matter:
Dear Sir,

> Yours faithfully,

The social manner is:

Dear Canon,   *or*
Dear Canon ————,
                                Yours sincerely,

Address of envelope in both cases—
                        The Revd. Canon ————.

Minor canons are addressed as other members of the clergy, with no special title.

PREBENDARIES

are addressed and referred to as Prebendary ————.
The most formal manner of address in writing is:

Reverend Sir,
                I have the honour to be, Reverend Sir,
                        Your obedient servant,

  Less formally, but not socially or on a church matter:

Dear Sir,
                                Yours faithfully,

The social manner is:

Dear Prebendary,   *or*
Dear Prebendary ————,
                                Yours sincerely,

Address of envelope in both cases—
                        The Revd. Prebendary ————.

OTHER MEMBERS OF THE CLERGY

There is no difference in style of addressing the remaining ranks, although beneficed clergymen are usually called in speech either The Vicar or The Rector. But it is definitely wrong to speak or refer to a clergyman as the

Revd. Smith. Initials or name must *always* be used. The style Revd. Mr Smith was common in England within living memory, but its use is now confined to North America, where it is correct. (It may still be used here, if initials or Christian name are not known.) When the name of a clergyman and his wife appear together, the correct form is:

The Revd. A. B. and Mrs. Smith.

The most formal manner of address in writing is:

Reverend Sir,   *or*
Sir,

I beg to remain, Reverend Sir (or Sir),
Your obedient servant,

Less formally:

Dear Sir,

Yours faithfully,

The social manner is:

Dear Mr Smith, *or* Dear Rector (or Vicar),
Yours sincerely,

Address of envelope in both cases—
The Revd. A.B. Smith.

TITLED CLERICS

A temporal title is always preceded in writing by the spiritual one.

Examples.—The Right Revd. and Right Hon. The Lord Bishop of London.
The Revd. Lord John Smith.
The Revd. The Hon. David Jones.
The Revd. Sir John Bull, Bt.

No ordained priest of the Church can receive the accolade of knighthood, but in some cases an appointment to an order of knighthood is made which carries the designation (e.g. K.C.V.O.) without the title. The wife of a priest so honoured is not styled or addressed Lady.

MEMBERS OF ANGLICAN RELIGIOUS COMMUNITIES

The head of a community is addressed in writing as The Right Revd. The Lord Abbot, The Revd. (or The Revd. Father) Superior, or The Revd. The Prior, according to his office as head of that community. The initials of the community (should it use them) are added after the name. The letter should begin Dear Father Abbot (or Prior or Superior).

An ordained member of a community is addressed, for example:

The Revd. (or The Revd. Father) A. B. Smith, S.S.J.E.
The Revd. (or The Revd. Father) J. L. Read, D.D., C.R.

A lay member is addressed:

> Brother John,   *or*
> Brother John Green.

Benedictines, whether ordained or lay, are addressed as Dom:

> The Revd. Dom James Martin, O.S.B.,   *or*
> Dom James Martin, O.S.B., if a lay member.

The head of a community for women is addressed as The Revd. Mother Superior, or The Revd. The Prioress, according to her office. Ordinary members of the community are addressed by their Christian, or by their Christian and surnames, according to the custom of the community, preceded by Sister and followed by the initials of the community.

CHANCELLORS

are the judges of the Episcopal Courts and the principal lay officers of the respective dioceses. They are usually, but not invariably, barristers. The title is used only in connection with their official duties. By the clergy and others within the diocese they should be called in speech Mr Chancellor, or, more familiarly, Chancellor. When sitting in court, Sir, Worshipful Sir (*not* Your Worship) and The Learned Chancellor are correct. In writing, Sir, Dear Sir, or, less formally, Dear Mr Chancellor, should be used.

The envelope should be addressed—

The Worshipful Chancellor Smith,   *or*
The Worshipful Thomas Smith,   *or*
The Worshipful Sir Thomas Smith (if a knight).

If the chancellor is a Q.C. the abbreviation should be added after the name.

A lady will be addressed as Worshipful Madam, or Madam Chancellor.

THE ROMAN CATHOLIC CHURCH

It should be understood that the following rules have no legal foundation in this country. Roman Catholic archbishops and bishops have no claim to territorial titles or to the use of the salutations Your Grace or My Lord, and such modes of address are not permitted in official documents and circles. But unofficially and within the Roman Catholic community this chapter holds good.

THE POPE

is the supreme head on earth of the Roman Catholic Church, and is personally addressed and referred to as Your Holiness or His Holiness.

The formal manner in English is:

Your Holiness,
    I have the honour to remain,
        Your Holiness's most devoted and obedient child,

or

Most Holy Father,
        Your Holiness's most humble child,

A non-Roman Catholic may subscribe himself "servant" and not "child".

Address of envelope—
        His Holiness The Pope.

Letters addressed to the Pope would normally go through ecclesiastical channels, and if written in English would be translated into Latin.

CARDINALS

are addressed and referred to in speech both formally and socially as Your Eminence and His Eminence.

The most formal manner of address in writing is:

My Lord Cardinal,   *or*
Your Eminence,
    I have the honour to remain, my Lord Cardinal,
        Your Eminence's devoted and obedient child,

Less formally:

Your Eminence,
        I remain, Your Eminence,
          Yours faithfully,

The social manner in writing is:

Dear Cardinal ————,

>> Yours sincerely,

Address of envelope in each case—
>> His Eminence Cardinal ————.

CARDINAL ARCHBISHOPS

Rules as for CARDINALS apply here, excepting as to the address of envelope, which should be:

His Eminence The Cardinal Archbishop of ————.

or, preferably,

His Eminence Cardinal ————, Archbishop of————,

since the dignity of Cardinal is personal, and not attached to the office of Archbishop. The same rule should be followed for Cardinals who are Bishops.

ARCHBISHOPS

are addressed and referred to in speech both formally and socially as Your Grace and His Grace. The most formal manner of address in writing is:

My Lord Archbishop,   *or*
Your Grace,

>> I have the honour to remain, my Lord Archbishop,
>> Your Grace's devoted and obedient child,

Less formally:

Your Grace,

>> Yours faithfully,

The social manner is:

Dear Archbishop,

>> Yours sincerely,

Address of envelope—
>   His Grace The Archbishop of ————,   *or*
> The   Most   Revd.   James   Smith,   Archbishop   of
> ————.

Retired archbishops are addressed by name:
>   The Most Revd. Archbishop Smith.

Official form within the British Commonwealth:

Most Reverend Sir,
>   I (We) have the honour to be,
>   Your faithful servant(s),

>   *Address of envelope—*
>   The Most Revd. Archbishop Brown.

BISHOPS

The manner of address in speech both formally and socially is My Lord and His Lordship. The most formal manner of address in writing is:

My Lord,   *or*
My Lord Bishop,
>   I have the honour to remain,
>   Your Lordship's obedient servant (or child),

Less formally:

My Lord,
>   Yours faithfully,

The social manner is:

Dear Bishop,
>   Yours sincerely,

>   *Address of envelope in both cases—*
>   The Right Revd. James Smith, Bishop of
>   ————, *or*
>   His Lordship The Bishop of ————.

Retired bishops are addressed by name:
>The Right Revd. Bishop Smith.

Official form within the British Commonwealth:

Right Reverend Sir,
>I (We) have the honour to be,
>Your faithful servant(s),

Address of envelope—
>The Right Revd. Bishop Brown.

IRISH BISHOPS

The foregoing rules apply, except that the envelope is addressed:

>The Most Revd. The Bishop of ————.

Bishops in other English-speaking countries are customarily also addressed as Most Revd.

BISHOPS COADJUTOR

are appointed to assist a bishop or archbishop, and will normally succeed him on his retirement. They are addressed as bishops, using the personal name:

>The Right Revd. William Flynn, Bishop Coadjutor
>   of ————.

BISHOPS AUXILIARY

are also appointed to assist an archbishop or a bishop, but without the expectation of succession. They are addressed in the same way as a bishop coadjutor, adding their office on the envelope:

>The Right Revd. John Haines, Bishop Auxiliary
>   of ————.

Titular Sees

Foregoing rules for Archbishops and Bishops apply, excepting as to envelopes, which are addressed:

The Most Revd. Archbishop Brown.
The Right Revd. (or Most Revd.) Bishop Brown.
It is unnecessary to refer to the titular see.

Provosts

are addressed in speech as Provost ————. The most formal manner of address in writing is:

Very Reverend Sir,
   I have the honour to remain, Very Reverend Sir,
     Your obedient servant,

 Less formally:

Dear Sir,
     Yours faithfully,

 The social manner of address in writing is:

Dear Provost ————, *or*
Dear Provost,
     Yours sincerely,

 Address of envelope—
   The Very Revd. Provost ————.

Canons

Canons are addressed and referred to in speech as Canon ————. The most formal manner of address in writing is:

Very Reverend Sir,
   I have the honour to remain, Very Reverend Sir,
     Your obedient servant,

Less formally:

Dear Sir,
                          Yours faithfully,

The social manner of address in writing is:

Dear Canon ————,   *or*
Dear Canon,
                          Yours sincerely,

Address of envelope—
            The Very Revd. Canon ————.

If he is a Monsignore, this is added: The Very Revd.
Monsignor (Canon) ————. Both titles may be used,
but it is unnecessary.

MONSIGNORI

are addressed and referred to in speech, both formally
and socially, as Monsignor Smith, or as Monsignore.
They may be Protonotaries, Domestic Prelates, Privy
Chamberlains, or Honorary Chamberlains of His Holiness
the Pope. The most formal manner of address is:

Reverend Sir,
        I have the honour to remain, Reverend Sir,
                          Your devoted and obedient servant,

Less formally:

Reverend Sir,
                          Yours faithfully,

The social manner of address is:

Dear Monsignore,   *or*
Dear Monsignor Smith,
                          Yours sincerely,

Address of envelope—
The Revd. Mgr. Smith, *or*
The Revd. Monsignore.

ABBOTS

Abbots are addressed and referred to in speech as Father Abbot. The most formal manner of address in writing is:

My Lord Abbot, *or*
Right Reverend Abbot ————, *or*
Right Reverend Father,

   I beg to remain, my Lord Abbot (or alternatives),
     Your devoted and obedient servant,

Less formally:

My Lord Abbot,

     Yours faithfully,

The social manner of address is:

Dear Father Abbot,

    Yours sincerely,

Address of envelope—
The Right Revd. The Abbot of Thornton.

PROVINCIALS

are addressed and referred to in speech as Father ————.

The most formal manner of address in writing is:

Very Reverend Father,

   I beg to remain, Very Reverend Father,
     Your devoted and obedient child,

Less formally:

Very Reverend Father,

    Yours faithfully,

The social manner of address is:

Dear Father ————, *or*
Dear Father Provincial,

> Yours sincerely,

Address of envelope—
The Very Revd. Father ————, *or*
The Very Revd. Father Provincial (with distinguishing
   initials of his order).

BENEDICTINES

Are called Dom. The formal manner of address in
writing is:

Dear Reverend Father,

while the social manner of address is:

Dear Dom Henry Smith, *or*
Dear Dom Henry,

> *Address of envelope—*
> The Revd. Dom H. Smith, O.S.B.

PRIESTS

are addressed and referred to in speech as Father ————.

The most formal manner of address in writing is:

Dear Reverend Father,

> Your devoted and obedient child,

Less formally:

Dear Reverend Father,

> Yours faithfully,

The social manner of address in writing is:

Dear Father ————,

> Yours sincerely,

Address of envelope—
>The Revd. Father ————.

WOMEN IN RELIGIOUS COMMUNITIES

The head of a community may be called Abbess, Prioress, Superior, or Reverend Mother. She will be addressed according to her office, with the addition of the letters of her order:

The Lady Abbess,
The Reverend Mother Prioress,
The Reverend Mother,
The Mother Superior,
The Sister Superior.

Letters should begin:

Dear Lady Abbess,
Dear Reverend Mother,
Dear Sister Superior.

Other members of the order are addressed as The Reverend Sister, with Christian name, or Christian and surname, according to the custom of the order, and with the letters of the order.

THE CHURCH OF SCOTLAND

THE LORD HIGH COMMISSIONER TO THE GENERAL ASSEMBLY

is addressed and referred to as Your Grace and His Grace during his term of office. The formal manner of address in writing is:

Your Grace,
>I have the honour to remain,
>Your Grace's most devoted and obedient servant,

Address of envelope—
> His Grace The Lord High Commissioner.

The social manner of address is the same, viz. Your Grace, etc., except when the office is held by a member of the Royal Family, in which case the formal and social address may be either Your Royal Highness or Your Grace.

THE MODERATOR

is addressed in speech as Moderator, or as Dr. ———— (or Mr ————, as the case may be). The most formal manner of address in writing is:

Right Reverend Sir,
> I beg to remain, Right Reverend Sir,
>> Your obedient servant,

Less formally:

Dear Sir, *or*
Dear Moderator,
> Yours faithfully,

Address of envelope—
The Right Revd. The Moderator of The General Assembly of The Church of Scotland.

The social manner of address in writing is:

Dear Moderator, *or*
Dear Dr. (or Mr) Smith,
> Yours sincerely,

Address of envelope—
The Right Revd. The Moderator of The Church of Scotland.

EX-MODERATORS

These dignitaries are designated The Very Reverend.

The most formal manner of address in writing is:

Very Reverend Sir,

            I beg to remain, Very Reverend Sir,

                 Your obedient servant,

  Less formally:

Dear Sir, *or*
Dear Minister,

           Yours faithfully,

  The social manner of address in writing is:

Dear Dr. (or Mr) Smith,

         Yours sincerely,

  Address of envelope in both cases—
    The Very Revd. Albert Smith (and if a Dr.), D.D.

Dean of the Thistle and Chapel Royal

Rules as for Deans of the Church of England apply here (*see* p. 120).

Other Members of the Clergy

Rules as for the Church of England apply (*see* p. 123), excepting that the titles of Vicar and Rector are not used. A minister in a regular parochial charge is often called The Minister (of the parish) or the Parish Minister, and envelopes are addressed The Minister of ————.

OTHER FREE CHURCHES

Ministers of the Free Churches are addressed formally:

Dear Sir, *or*
Dear Minister,

           Yours faithfully,
(For women Ministers, Dear Madam,).

The social manner of address in writing is:

Dear Mr (or Dr.) Smith,
                        Yours sincerely,

Address of envelope—
        The Revd. Matthew Smith,   *or*
        The Revd. Margaret Smith.

"The Revd. Smith" is in all cases incorrect, and "Revd. Smith" even more so.

THE EASTERN CHURCH

PATRIARCHS

are personally addressed and referred to as Your Holiness or His Holiness. The style of address in writing is:

Your Holiness,
                I have the honour to be, Sir,
                        Your Holiness's obedient servant,

Address of envelope—
                His Holiness The Patriarch.

METROPOLITANS

are personally addressed and referred to as Your Grace and His Grace. The style of address in writing is:

Your Grace,
                I am, Sir,
                        Your Grace's obedient servant,

Address of envelope—
        His Beatitude The Metropolitan of ————.

ARCHBISHOPS AND BISHOPS

as for Anglican Archbishops and Bishops (*see* pp. 114 and 117).

ARCHIMANDRITES

Archimandrites are addressed and referred to in speech as Right Reverend Father. The formal manner of address in writing is:

Right Reverend Father,
> I beg to remain, Right Reverend Father,
>> Your obedient servant,

The social manner is:

Dear Father,
>> Yours sincerely,

THE ABUNA OF ABYSSINIA

is personally addressed and referred to as Your Grace and His Grace. The style of address in writing is:

Your Grace,
> I am, Sir,
>> Your Grace's obedient servant,

Address of envelope—
>> His Beatitude The Abuna.

OTHER DENOMINATIONS

As a matter of courtesy, rules as for OTHER CLERGY of the Church of England apply (*see* p. 123).

THE JEWISH SYNAGOGUE

MINISTERS

are addressed and referred to in speech as Mr Cohen or Dr. Cohen, according to degree. The most formal manner of address in writing is:

Reverend and dear Sir,
> I am, Reverend Sir,
>> Your obedient servant,

Less formally:

Dear Sir,

> Yours faithfully,

The social manner of address is:

Dear Mr (or Dr.) Cohen,

> Yours sincerely,

Address of envelope in each case—
> The Revd. A. Cohen, *or*
> The Revd. Dr. A. Cohen.

RABBIS

are addressed and referred to in speech as Rabbi Cohen
The most formal manner of address in writing is:

Reverend and dear Sir,

> I am, Reverend Sir,
> > Your obedient servant,

Less formally:

Dear Sir,

> Yours faithfully,

The social manner of address is:

Dear Rabbi Cohen,

> Yours sincerely,

Address of envelope—
> The Revd. Rabbi A. Cohen.

RABBI DOCTORS

are addressed and referred to in speech as Dr. Cohen.

The social manner of address is:

Dear Dr. Cohen,

> Yours sincerely,

Address of envelope—
> The Revd. Rabbi Dr. A. Cohen.

THE CHIEF RABBI

is addressed and referred to in speech as Chief Rabbi.
The most formal manner of address in writing is:

Very Reverend and dear Sir,

I am, Very Reverend Sir,
Your obedient servant,

Less formally:

Dear Sir,

Yours faithfully,

The social manner of address in writing is:

Dear Chief Rabbi,

Yours sincerely,

Address of envelope—

The Very Revd. The Chief Rabbi,   *or*
The Chief Rabbi Dr. J. Cohen.

THE ROYAL NAVY

THIS is the senior fighting service. Titles which have duplicates in the Army rank higher in the Navy. In these cases, and indeed for all ranks below Rear-Admiral, the words Royal Navy, or more usually in ordinary correspondence the abbreviation R.N., will be added after the name, and any decorations and orders. All ranks above that of sub-lieutenant are addressed and referred to in speech by their service title (unless they possess a higher title otherwise). Decorations and honours should never be omitted from envelopes. A few general rules are given below.

ADMIRALS OF THE FLEET

Address of envelopes both formally and socially:
Admiral of The Fleet Lord (or any other title) ———.
In other respects according to peerage or other rank.

ADMIRALS
VICE-ADMIRALS
REAR-ADMIRALS

All are addressed in speech as Admiral ———.
Only on envelopes are the graded titles used.
The most formal manner of address in writing is:

Sir,
> I have the honour to remain, Sir,
> > Your obedient servant,

Less formally:

Dear Sir,
> Yours faithfully,

The social manner is by his title if he has one, otherwise:
Dear Admiral Flint,
although officers of this rank may express a preference for being addressed by rank rather than by title; if so their preference should be followed.

COMMODORES

This rank is held by senior captains in special appointments. The title is used in speech both formally and socially. The most formal manner is:

Sir,
I have the honour to be, Sir,
Your obedient servant,

Less formally:
Dear Sir,
Yours faithfully,

The social manner is:
Dear Commodore Beal,
Yours sincerely,

Address of envelope in every case—
Commodore A. Beal, Royal Navy.

CAPTAINS

The title is used in speech both formally and socially.
The most formal manner of address in writing is:

Sir,
I have the honour to be, Sir,
Your obedient servant,

Less formally:
Dear Sir,
Yours faithfully,

The social manner of address in writing is:
Dear Captain Birch,
Yours sincerely,

Address of envelope in both cases—
> Captain A. B. Birch, Royal Navy.

COMMANDERS

This title is used both formally and socially in speech.

Address of envelope in both cases—
> Commander C. D. Bartlett, Royal Navy.

LIEUTENANT-COMMANDERS

are addressed in speech as Commander. Only on envelopes is the graded title used.

LIEUTENANTS

are addressed officially in speech as Lieutenant and socially as Mr.

Address of envelope in either case—
> Lieutenant G. H. Crane, Royal Navy.

SUB-LIEUTENANTS
MIDSHIPMEN
CADETS

All are addressed in social and official speech as Mr. Official and social envelopes are addressed:

> Sub.-Lieut. I. J. Drake, Royal Navy.
> Midshipman K. L. Blake, Royal Navy.
> Cadet M. N. Hawke, Royal Navy.

RETIRED OFFICERS

A retired officer should be addressed in exactly the same way as one on the active list, except that the abbreviation 'Rtd' should be added whenever it is necessary to indicate the fact. For instance, a private letter should be addressed without the suffix, but a letter to a retired officer working, say in the Ministry of Defence, or for a ship-builder, should add 'Rtd'.

TITLED OFFICERS

A hereditary or conferred title is preceded by the naval one.

Examples.—Admiral Sir Norman Blake.

Captain The Hon. Norman Birch, Royal Navy.

CHAPLAINS

The Chaplain of the Fleet is an Archdeacon, and is addressed accordingly. The envelope may be addressed to The Chaplain of the Fleet, or with this designation added to the name. Other chaplains are addressed as clergymen with the words Royal Navy attached to their name.

DECORATIONS

Abbreviations are used immediately after the name thus:

Captain O. P. Hawke, D.S.O., Royal Navy.

Lieut. A. R. Crane, D.S.C., Royal Navy.

They should, of course, never be omitted.

GENERAL LIST, MEDICAL AND INSTRUCTOR OFFICERS

The foregoing rules apply to all officers on the General List (i.e. Seaman, Engineering, Electrical Engineering, and Supply & Secretariat specialists). Similar rules apply to Medical and Instructor Officers, except that their ranks should, in speech and writing, be prefixed by the name of their branch:

e.g. Surgeon-Commander S. T. Brice.

ROYAL MARINES

Officers of the Royal Marines have Army ranks, and are addressed in the same way, with the letters R.M. following the name if their rank is Lieutenant-Colonel or below. (*See* p. 151).

THE ARMY

ALL ranks above that of lieutenant are addressed and referred to in speech by their service title (unless they possess a higher one otherwise). Decorations and honours should never be omitted from envelopes.

FIELD-MARSHALS

Address of envelope, both formally and socially:

Field-Marshal Lord (or any other title) —————.

In other respects according to peerage or other rank.

GENERALS
LIEUTENANT-GENERALS
MAJOR-GENERALS

All are addressed in speech as General —————. Only on envelopes are the graded titles used. The formal manner of address in writing is Sir, the social manner is Dear General Sands, or by his title if he has one, according to his preference.

BRIGADIERS

Addressed in speech and on envelopes as Brigadier Blank. The formal manner of address in writing is Sir, the social manner is Dear Brigadier Blank.

COLONELS

Addressed in speech and on envelopes as Colonel Howe. The formal manner of address in writing is Sir, and the social manner Dear Colonel Howe.

LIEUTENANT-COLONELS

are addressed in speech as Colonel. Only on envelopes is the graded title used. The regiment is added after the name, and any distinctions he may possess, thus:

Lieut.-Colonel H. Newcombe, D.S.O., R.H.A.

The formal manner of address in writing is Sir, the social manner Dear Colonel Newcombe.

MAJORS
CAPTAINS

Addressed in speech as Major Shaw and Captain Shaw respectively. The formal manner of address in writing is Sir, the social manner Dear Major (or Captain) Shaw.

Address of envelope—
Major (or Captain) E. Shaw, 11th Hussars.

LIEUTENANTS
SECOND-LIEUTENANTS

Addressed in speech as Mr. The formal manner in writing is Sir, the social manner Dear Mr Fry.

Address of official and service envelopes—
Lieut. (or 2nd Lieut.) T. W. Fry, 2nd Life Guards.

Address of social envelope—
T. W. Fry, Esq., 2nd Life Guards.

RETIRED OFFICERS

do not have a regiment appended to their names. It used to be the practice for retired officers under the rank of Major to drop their title, but now a retired captain will be addressed by his rank if he chooses to use it.

CHAPLAINS

The Chaplain-General to the Forces ranks as major-general, and there are four classes below him, ranking respectively as colonels, lieut.-colonels, majors, and captains, but they are addressed in speech and in writing according to their rank as clergymen. The Chaplain-General himself is an Archdeacon. Envelopes to the chaplain-general are addressed To The Chaplain-General of the Forces, and other chaplains have the abbreviation C.F. or S.C.F. added to the name. In no circumstances should military titles be used.

TITLED OFFICERS

A hereditary or conferred title is preceded by the military one, as

> Colonel Lord John Bull, 10th Lancers.
> General Sir James Horn.

DECORATIONS

Abbreviations are shown immediately after the name, thus:

> Colonel Newcombe, V.C.
> T. W. Fry, Esq., M.C., 2nd Life Guards.

They should, of course, never be omitted.

THE ROYAL AIR FORCE

THE rules relating to the Navy and the Army apply in general. All service titles are used officially, but service titles below that of Flight Lieutenant are not used socially. Decorations and honours should never be omitted from envelopes, and are placed immediately after the name. The abbreviation R.A.F. is placed after decorations and honours below the rank of Air Commodore.

MARSHALS OF THE ROYAL AIR FORCE

Address all envelopes, both formally and socially:

Marshal of the Royal Air Force Lord (or any other title)————.

In other respects according to peerage or other title.

AIR CHIEF MARSHALS
AIR MARSHALS
AIR VICE-MARSHALS

Addressed in speech as Air Marshal, but the professional title is never further abbreviated. Only on envelopes are graded professional titles used. The formal manner of address in writing is Sir, the social manner in writing is Dear Air Marshal (or Air Marshal Smith), or by his title if he has one, according to his preference.

AIR COMMODORES

Addressed formally in speech and in writing as Air Commodore Jones. Socially addressed in speech as Air Commodore Jones. The professional title is never abbreviated in social usage. Air Commodores and above are officially graded as "air officers".

GROUP CAPTAINS
WING COMMANDERS
SQUADRON LEADERS

These senior officer grades are addressed by their service titles, which—in the social manner—are never abbreviated. May be spoken of as the Group Captain, or Group Captain White, or directly addressed Squadron Leader or Squadron Leader Black.

FLIGHT LIEUTENANTS

Addressed by service title which—in the social manner —is never abbreviated. Spoken of as Flight Lieutenant Brown, but not as Flight Lieutenant.

FLYING OFFICERS
PILOT OFFICERS

The service titles are used only for official purposes. Social manner of address is Mr. Gray. Envelopes should be addressed:

A. B. Gray Esq., D.F.C. (or other decorations if any), R.A.F.

CHAPLAINS

The Chaplain-in-Chief, Royal Air Force has the relative rank of Air Vice-Marshal, and other Royal Air Force Chaplains have ranks relative to Group Captain down to Flight Lieutenant.

Chaplains are, however, known and addressed both officially and otherwise according to their ecclesiastical titles, which for the Chaplain-in-Chief is Archdeacon, and not by their relative status in the Royal Air Force. For example, an envelope should be addressed:

The Reverend A. Green, R.A.F. — and not as Squadron Leader the Rev. A. Green.

COMPARATIVE RANKS IN H.M. FIGHTING FORCES

ROYAL NAVY	ARMY	ROYAL AIR FORCE
ADMIRAL OF THE FLEET	FIELD-MARSHAL	MARSHAL OF THE ROYAL AIR FORCE
ADMIRAL	GENERAL	AIR CHIEF MARSHAL
VICE-ADMIRAL	LIEUTENANT-GENERAL	AIR MARSHAL
REAR-ADMIRAL	MAJOR-GENERAL	AIR VICE-MARSHAL
COMMODORE	BRIGADIER	AIR COMMODORE
CAPTAIN	COLONEL	GROUP CAPTAIN
COMMANDER	LIEUTENANT-COLONEL	WING COMMANDER
LIEUTENANT-COMMANDER	MAJOR	SQUADRON LEADER
LIEUTENANT	CAPTAIN	FLIGHT LIEUTENANT
SUB-LIEUTENANT	LIEUTENANT	FLYING OFFICER
	SECOND LIEUTENANT	PILOT OFFICER

In the Royal Marines ranks compare with Navy ranks as Army ranks do down to Colonel; but Colonel and Lieutenant-Colonel R.M. are both the equivalent of a Captain R.N., and a Major R.M. of a Commander R.N., and so on down.

THE WOMEN'S SERVICES

THE comparative ranks in the Women's Services are given in the table below. Their use is, in general, the same as for Military, Naval and Air Force ranks, except that Madam is used instead of Sir (Ma'am would ordinarily be used in speaking).

W.R.A.C.	W.R.N.S.	W.R.A.F.
MAJOR-GENERAL	CHIEF COMMANDANT	AIR MARSHAL
BRIGADIER	COMMANDANT	AIR COMMODORE
COLONEL	SUPERINTENDENT	GROUP CAPTAIN
LIEUT.-COLONEL	CHIEF OFFICER	WING COMMANDER
MAJOR	FIRST OFFICER	SQUADRON LEADER
CAPTAIN	SECOND OFFICER	FLIGHT LIEUTENANT
LIEUTENANT	THIRD OFFICER	FLYING OFFICER
2ND LIEUTENANT	—	PILOT OFFICER

LAW, DIPLOMATIC
AND GOVERNMENT

THE various titles and offices are given alphabetically.

AGENTS-GENERAL

These are the representatives in London of the provincial or state governments (not the Federal Governments) of Canada or Australia. They are addressed according to their own name and rank, with their office following the name on an envelope.

ALDERMEN

Addressed during office as Alderman. Official letters begin:

Dear Sir,

Social letters begin:

Dear Alderman,   *or*   Dear Alderman Jones.

Address of envelope—
>   Alderman J. Jones.

If an Alderman possesses another title this should of course be used; in such cases Alderman precedes other designations, as also with Miss or Mrs.

>   Alderman Sir Joseph Jones.
>   Alderman Mrs. Jones.

It is not however necessary to multiply titles in this way, and it should be avoided except when writing to the Alderman in that capacity.

AMBASSADORS

The formal and social manner of address in speech is Your Excellency or Sir. The formal manner of address in writing is:

My Lord (or Sir, according to rank),
    I have the honour to be, my Lord (or Sir),
        Your Excellency's obedient servant,

The social manner in writing is:

Dear Mr Whitby (Sir Charles, or according to rank),
        Yours sincerely,

Address of envelope (formal or social)—
    His Excellency Mr Charles Whitby, C.M.G.
      (Sir Charles Whitby, G.C.B.),
        H.M. Embassy,
(Esq. is not used with His Excellency.)

Ambassadors' wives do not share their husbands' official title of Excellency, although it is still accorded them by courtesy in some countries, and the usage has not entirely ceased in others.

ATTORNEYS-GENERAL

are addressed in speech according to their own name and rank. They are invariably Q.C.s and rules as for Queen's Counsel apply. On envelopes they may be addressed as The Attorney-General or by their name and rank.

BAILIES (of Scottish Burghs)

Addressed during office as Bailie. Social letters begin:

Dear Bailie Campbell,

Address of envelope—
    Bailie J. Campbell.

CHAIRMEN OF QUARTER SESSIONS

Courts of Quarter Sessions will be abolished when the Courts Act 1971 comes into force in 1972. Whole-time Chairmen and Deputy Chairmen of Courts of Quarter Sessions will then become Circuit Judges (*see* p. 159). Until then they are addressed in the same way as County Court Judges. Part-time Chairmen and Deputy Chairmen of Quarter Sessions are, so long as the appointment is made, addressed according to their own name and rank.

CHARGÉS D'AFFAIRES

usually take the place temporarily of ambassadors at embassies and of ministers at legations, while at a few posts the office is a permanent one. They rank below envoys-extraordinary in diplomatic circles, but the same rules apply.

CONSULS

Envelopes are addressed—

        To George Smith, Esq.,

            H.M. Agent and Consul-General, *or*

            H.M. Consul-General, *or*

            H.M. Consul, *or*

            H.M. Vice-Consul,

In all other respects as an Esquire (*see* p. 108).

COUNCILLORS

The same rules apply as for Aldermen (*see* p. 153).

DEPUTY LIEUTENANTS OF COUNTIES

are addressed in speech according to their own name and rank. For official letters the affix D.L. should be used (*see* pp. 170 and 171).

ENVOYS-EXTRAORDINARY AND MINISTERS-PLENIPOTENTIARY

rank below ambassadors, and are in charge of legations as ambassadors are of embassies. Rules as for AMBASSADORS apply (*see* p. 154), except that they are not styled "His Excellency"; the envelope would be addressed:

> J. Winter, Esq., C.B.E. (or other distinction),
> H.M. Minister,
> British Legation.

At present only two Ministers-Plenipotentiary are appointed, all other posts being upgraded to embassies. (*See also* Ministers (Diplomatic Service), p. 165 for "Minister" used as a rank.)

GOVERNORS-GENERAL
GOVERNORS
LIEUTENANT-GOVERNORS

Governors-General and Governors are called "His Excellency" while holding office and in their territories; the wives of Governors-General are also so addressed, but not the wives of Governors. The Lieutenant-Governors of Jersey, Guernsey and the Isle of Man have the same style; the Lieutenant-Governors of Canadian provinces are called "The Honourable" for life.

Envelopes are addressed—

> His Excellency Sir John ————, Governor-General of ——,
> His Excellency Mr J. H. ————, Governor and Commander-in-Chief of ————.

H.M. LIEUTENANTS OF COUNTIES. (*See* Lieutenants of Counties)

HIGH COMMISSIONERS

represent one country of the Commonwealth in another. They are in effect Ambassadors, and are addressed similarly.

Forms of address are as follows:

Formally:

> Your Excellency,
> > I have the honour to be,
> > > Your Excellency's obedient servant,

> His Excellency Mr
> > > The Honourable
> > > The Right Honourable
> > > (according to rank)

Informally:

> Dear High Commissioner,
> > Believe me,
> > > Dear High Commissioner,
> > > Yours sincerely,

> His Excellency Mr ————— (*as above*).

HONOURABLE

The title "The Honourable" is accorded in the Commonwealth and other English-speaking countries to holders of a number of public offices, including Ministers (or their equivalent), Judges, members of *some* legislative bodies, Governors or Lieutenant-Governors, and so on. It may be held for life or during tenure of office; within the scope of this book it is sufficient to say that the usage exists and should be followed where it appears; and that it is not usual to abbreviate "The Honorable" in the United States.

JUDGES OF THE HIGH COURT

are usually knighted on appointment. They are addressed and referred to as My Lord and Your (or His) Lordship on the Bench, in the precincts of the Court, and whenever they are being approached in their judicial capacity. The formal manner of address in writing is, according to circumstances, either My Lord or Sir.

The Address of the envelope is—
The Hon. Mr Justice Swift.

Queen's Counsel who are appointed High Court Judges no longer use the initials after their name.

In their private capacities they may be addressed in speech as "Mr Justice Smith", as "Judge", or as "Sir John", and in writing as:

The Hon. Mr Justice Swift, *or*
The Hon. Sir John Swift.

As with Circuit Judges (*see* p. 159), the second to be appointed of two High Court Judges with the same name will have chosen to be known by a forename in addition.

In 1965 the first woman Judge of the High Court was appointed. She was made a Dame of the Most Excellent Order of the British Empire on her appointment, and is addressed in Court as My Lady and Your (or Her) Ladyship.

The formal manner of address in writing is:

The Hon. Mrs Justice Lane.

Socially she may be addressed in speech as "Mrs Justice Lane" or as "Dame Elizabeth Lane". In writing she is addressed as:

The Hon. Dame Elizabeth Lane, D.B.E., *or*
The Hon. Mrs Justice Lane, D.B.E.

The prefix "The Honourable" and the style The Hon. Mr Justice are not retained after retirement.

JUDGES OF THE COUNTY COURT AND CIRCUIT JUDGES

With the coming into force of the Courts Act 1971 in 1972, the office of County Court Judge is replaced by that of Circuit Judge; the form of address remains the same. They are addressed and referred to on the Bench as Your Honour and His Honour. Socially they are addressed and referred to in conversation as Judge or Judge Jones. Letters are addressed:

Dear Judge,   *or*   Dear Judge Jones.

Address of envelope both socially and officially—

His Honour Judge Jones.

Queen's Counsel who are appointed Circuit Judges continue to use the initials Q.C. after their names.

Where two judges have the same (or even a very similar) surname, the second to be appointed will choose to be known by one of his Christian names as well as his surname; for example, Mr Henry Roberts Jones is made a Circuit Judge, and (because there is already a Judge, or a Mr Justice Jones) is known as His Honour Judge Roberts Jones.

The title His Honour is now retained after retirement, omitting the word Judge, and adding the Christian name or initials; so that the address of the envelope is:

His Honour Henry Jones.

JUDGES OVERSEAS

Judges of the High Courts or Supreme Courts of Commonwealth countries or overseas territories are addressed during office as:

The Honourable The Chief Justice,   *or*
The Hon. Mr. Justice ————.

The Chief Justice of Canada bears the title "Right Honourable" for life, and other judges of Commonwealth countries may be Privy Counsellors, when they will be addressed as Right Hon. also.

JUSTICES OF THE PEACE

Addressed on the Bench as Your Worship, and by letter socially as an Esquire (*see* p. 108), or according to rank. When writing to a Justice of the Peace in his official capacity (but only then), the affix J.P. should be used (*see* pp. 170 and 171).

LADY MAYORESSES

Rules as for wives of Lord Mayors apply (*see* p. 162).

LAW LORDS. (*See* LIFE PEERS, p. 43.)

LIEUTENANTS OF COUNTIES

are addressed according to their rank, e.g.

His Grace The Duke of Middlesex, K.G.,
H.M. Lieutenant for ————.

If he is a commoner the form is:
A. Smith, Esq.,
H.M. Lieutenant for ————.

In England the title Lord Lieutenant is a mere colloquialism and has no official foundation. In Scotland Lords Lieutenant are appointed by the Queen for all counties. In Northern Ireland the title is always H.M. Lieutenant, and the abbreviation H.M.L. is used after the name.

LORD ADVOCATE OF SCOTLAND

Formerly always My Lord, etc.; but latterly, probably from ceasing to be on the Bench, frequently as Sir; but is socially addressed as Lord Advocate, and in writing Dear Lord Advocate. He may be a member of the House of Lords or of the House of Commons, but need not be either; he is always a Privy Counsellor.

Envelopes are addressed—
>The Right Hon. The Lord Advocate.

LORD OF APPEAL-IN-ORDINARY

and his wife and children. Rules as for BARONS and BARONESSES apply (*see* pp. 83 to 89).

LORD CHAMBERLAIN

is addressed according to rank and title.

LORD CHANCELLOR

The Lord Chancellor is addressed and referred to in speech and writing according to his rank in the peerage. Envelopes are addressed both formally and socially:

>The Right Hon. The Lord Chancellor.

LORD CHIEF JUSTICE

If a peer he is addressed and referred to accordingly. Otherwise as a Judge (*see* p. 158).

Envelopes are addressed both formally and socially—
>The Right Hon. The Lord Chief Justice of England.

LORD JUSTICE OF APPEAL

Addressed and referred to as My Lord and His

Lordship and by professional and semi-professional or semi-official correspondents as

Dear Lord Justice.

Envelopes are addressed—
> The Right Hon. The Lord Justice ————.

LORD LIEUTENANTS OF COUNTIES. (*See* Lieutenants of Counties.)

LORD MAYORS

The Lord Mayors of Belfast, Cardiff, Dublin, London, and York, and of the Australian cities of Adelaide, Brisbane, Hobart, Melbourne, Sydney, and Perth are entitled to the style Right Hon. while they are in office. This is, however, only an official and not a personal prefix, and it is used only with the title "Lord Mayor" and not with the Lord Mayor's own name; it is incorrect to address such a Lord Mayor as, for example, "The Right Hon. Richard Whittington". Their wives (or the lady acting as Lady Mayoress) do not share the honour of the style Right Hon.

The formal mode of address both in speech and writing is My Lord and My Lady, while socially they are addressed according to their own name and rank excepting on the envelope.

Address of envelope, formally and socially—
The Right Hon. The Lord Mayor of ————.
The Lady Mayoress of ————.

The Mayors of certain other cities also are designated "Lord Mayors", and are addressed according to these rules, except as to envelope, which should be addressed

The Right Worshipful The Lord Mayor of ————.
The Lady Mayoress of ————,

The form of address does not vary when the Lord Mayor is a lady.

LORD PRIVY SEAL

is addressed according to his own name and title.

LORD PROVOSTS

are addressed and referred to as My Lord and His Lordship.

Envelopes are addressed—
> The Lord Provost of ————,

but the Lord Provost of Edinburgh is entitled to the words "The Right Hon." in front of his name, and the Lord Provost of Glasgow is known as "The Right Hon. the Lord Provost of Glasgow" and socially referred to as The Lord Provost; in social address Lord Provost, not (except in historical comparison) "Lord Provost Campbell", and addressed as The Lord Provost of ————. Letters begin

> Dear Lord Provost.

Their wives do not share the title, though there is a recent tendency to refer to them as The Lady Provost, which has led to such incorrect descriptions as "Lord Provost Campbell and the Lady Provost of ———— —", which should be avoided.

LORD OF SESSION

is a Judge of the Court of Session (or Senator of the College of Justice), of Scotland, who upon elevation to the Bench is styled for life The Hon. Lord, with his surname or a territorial name according to his choice. This is a title of judicial office, and not a peerage.

Envelopes are addressed—
> The Hon. Lord ——————.

His wife is addressed in writing as Lady ——————, and in other respects as the wife of a Baron (*see* p. 83), but without the prefix "Right Hon." Their children have no title. If a Lord of Session is also a Privy Counsellor he is of course addressed as The Right Hon. Lord ——————. The Lord Justice-General and the Lord Justice-Clerk of Scotland are Lords of Session; they are Privy Counsellors, and are always addressed by their office:

> The Right Hon. the Lord Justice-General,
> The Right Hon. the Lord Justice-Clerk.

Upon giving up this office they revert to the style of a Lord of Session who is a Privy Counsellor.

MAGISTRATES

See under Justices of the Peace (p. 160), and Stipendiary Magistrates (p. 167).

MASTER OF THE ROLLS

Rules as for Judges apply (*see* p. 158).

Address of envelope—
> The Right Hon. The Master of the Rolls,   *or*
> The Right Hon. (according to rank).

MASTERS OF THE SUPREME COURT
are addressed according to own name and rank.

MAYORS WHEN LADIES
are addressed as "Your Worship" or "Mr Mayor";

colloquially "Madam Mayor" is sometimes used, but this is not an established mode of address.

MAYORESSES

are addressed as "Mayoress", never "Your Worship", or "Mr Mayor", but if a Mayoress is a J.P. and is sitting on the Bench, the term "Your Worship" would of course be used when addressing the Bench.

MAYORS

Addressed as an Esquire (*see* p. 108), or according to own rank.

Envelopes are addressed—

If mayor of a city:
   The Right Worshipful The Mayor of ————.

If mayor of a borough:
   The Worshipful The Mayor of ————.

The Mayors of certain cities use the description "Lord Mayor" (*see* p. 162 under that heading).

MEMBERS OF PARLIAMENT

According to rank, with M.P. after the name.

MINISTERS (DIPLOMATIC SERVICE)

Ministers, Ministers (Economic), or Ministers (Commercial) may serve under the Ambassador in a large Embassy; but their title merely indicates their rank and they are not given any special form of address, as they would be if they were Ministers Plenipotentiary at the head of a Legation (*see* p. 156).

OFFICIAL REFEREES OF THE SUPREME COURT

Until the coming into force of the Courts Act 1971 in 1972, the title "His Honour" is inserted before the name.

His Honour Edward Brown, Q.C.

Thereafter they will become Circuit Judges (*see* p. 159).

PRIME MINISTERS

Are Privy Counsellors, and are so addressed, according to rank.

PROVOSTS OF SCOTTISH CITIES

As an Esquire (*see* p. 108), but referred to locally as The Provost, rather than "Mr X". But it should be noted that the Civic Heads of Edinburgh, Perth, Dundee, Aberdeen, and Glasgow are known as Lord Provost (*see* p. 163).

QUEEN'S COUNSEL

In all respects as an Esquire (or according to rank), with the initials Q.C. appended to the name on envelopes.

RECORDERS

Are addressed as an Esquire, or according to rank.

Recorders are barristers, and may be Queen's Counsel; if so the initials Q.C. should be added.

On the bench they are addressed as "Your Honour".

The Recorders of Liverpool and Manchester are also Judges of the Crown Courts in those cities. With the coming into force of the Courts Act 1971 in 1972, they will become Circuit Judges (*see* p. 159). Until then they are addressed as Judge ———— (not His Honour Judge ————), and in court are addressed as "My Lord" or "Your Lordship" as though they were Judges of the High Court.

SHERIFFS

are Judges of the Sheriff Courts in Scotland. There are twelve Sheriffs-Principal, and within each of their jurisdictions a number of Sheriffs. All are addressed in court as My Lord. Otherwise, officially and socially, as Sheriff ————, but the Sheriff-Principal is referred to as the Sheriff-Principal of ————, using the first territorial name of conjoined shrievalties, and is so announced.

STIPENDIARY MAGISTRATES

The same rules are followed as for Justices of the Peace, except that the letters J.P. are not used for stipendiary magistrates.

VICE-LIEUTENANTS

are addressed according to name and rank. The abbreviation V.L. following the name is not used.

ORDERS, DECORATIONS AND HONOURS

VICTORIA CROSS

The Victoria Cross is the most distinguished of all decorations, and is conferred for valour in all branches of the fighting services. Since 1920 it has been extended to include women. The abbreviation V.C. takes precedence of all other decorations and honours.

Other service decorations may be used in accordance with the table on page 169 in addressing a recipient in writing.

GEORGE CROSS

The George Cross is awarded for acts of great heroism or of conspicuous courage in extreme danger. It is intended primarily for civilians (both men and women), but awards are also made to members of the fighting services in actions for which military honours are not normally granted. The abbreviation G.C. follows V.C. but takes precedence of all other decorations and honours.

ORDER OF MERIT—O.M.

A very distinguished order, limited to twenty-four members, ranking in precedence immediately after Knights Grand Cross of the Order of the Bath.

ORDER OF THE COMPANIONS OF HONOUR—C.H.

An order limited to sixty-five members, for which women are equally eligible with men. It carries no titles, but holders use the initials C.H. after the name. It ranks in precedence after the 1st Class of the Order of the British Empire.

ORDERS EXCLUSIVELY FOR WOMEN

THE ROYAL ORDER OF VICTORIA AND ALBERT .	V.A.
THE IMPERIAL ORDER OF THE CROWN OF INDIA .	C.I.
THE ROYAL RED CROSS	R.R.C.

ORDER OF DECORATIONS AND HONOURS

The following table shows the correct order of the various degrees of Honour and Decorations of which the abbreviations are most commonly employed. A higher rank in an order includes the lower, i.e. it is never correct to put G.C.B., K.C.B., or K.C.M.G., C.M.G. All decorations and honours should be given.

(*N.B.*—For the various orders of Knighthood, *see* pp. 95 to 101).

V.C., G.C., K.G., K.T., K.P., G.C.B., O.M., G.C.S.I., G.C.M.G., G.C.I.E., C.I., G.C.V.O., G.B.E., C.H., K.C.B., K.C.S.I., K.C.M.G., K.C.I.E., K.C.V.O., K.B.E., C.B., C.S.I., C.M.G., C.I.E., C.V.O., C.B.E., D.S.O., M.V.O. (4th class), O.B.E., I.S.O., M.V.O. (5th class), M.B.E., R.R.C., D.S.C., M.C., D.F.C., A.F.C., A.R.R.C., A.M., D.C.M., C.G.M., G.M., D.S.M., M.M., D.F.M., A.F.M., B.E.M., Q.P.M., S.G.M., V.D., E.R.D., T.D., E.D., R.D., V.R.D.

(For ABBREVIATIONS, *see* pp. 1-23).

Various Commonwealth countries have instituted their own orders, which are awarded to their own citizens, and are indicated (in the British fashion) by post-nominal lettering. An example is the Order of Canada, in which three honours are conferred:

> Companion of the Order of Canada (C.C.);
> Officer of the Order of Canada (O.C.);
> Member of the Order of Canada (C.M.).

These letters, with others indicating membership of other Canadian orders, follow immediately after V.C. or G.C. in their appointed order, for Canadian citizens; and the letters of similar orders in other countries will likewise precede, for their own citizens, any others.

HONORIFIC AND OTHER AFFIXES

Honorific affixes, whether military decorations or not, should be appended in addressing formal letters; but those that are not honorific should be omitted. D.L. and J.P. are always omitted in social usage. In no circumstances do honorific initials (even V.C.) appear on visiting cards.

Affixes indicating professional qualification or official status should be used when addressing the correspondent in his professional or official capacity.

The order of lettering after the name (and after the abbreviations Bt. or Esq., if they apply), is fixed, and should be followed:

First, decorations and honours, in the order given on p. 169. They should not be omitted, if any letters are used at all, and in most circumstances it is preferable to include them in an address.

Second, the initials denoting certain Royal appointments. If for any reason it is necessary to include the initials P.C. they will come first, followed by A.D.C., Q.H.P., Q.H.S., Q.H.S.D.S., Q.H.N.S., Q.H.C.; but P.C. is nowadays never used on envelopes, and the other appointments, being short-term ones, are not normally used in ordinary correspondence, although they may be in official letters.

Third, University degrees (*see* p. 176).

Fourth, letters, other than university degrees, denoting medical qualifications; in normal correspondence, only those indicating fellowships or memberships would be used. F.R.C.P. and F.R.C.S. should always appear (in that order) if held, and so should the fellowships or memberships of the other institutions conferring postgraduate qualifications; medical precede surgical, which are followed by more specialized fellowships.

Fifth, the fellowships or memberships of learned societies, academies, or professional institutions. As a general rule, these should be shown in the order of the foundation of the societies, etc.; no distinction is made, in the order, between fellowships and memberships. The professional institutions whose highest rank was "member" are however changing this to "fellow"; except in professional correspondence, only these higher ranks would normally be shown. Those fellowships, etc., election to which is a distinction should be used in all correspondence: F.R.S., R.A. or A.R.A., R.S.A., F.B.A., are examples. Others which indicate merely that the fellow declares his interest in and support for the body concerned are used when the subject of his interest is the matter of the correspondence; and those which indicate professional eminence or qualification when writing on professional matters. The members of the fourteen bodies which make up the Council of Engineering Institutions are chartered engineers; they are entitled to use the letters C.Eng., which are placed immediately before the first fellowship or membership giving the right to use them:

J. B. MacTavish, Esq., C.Eng., M.I.C.E., F.I.Mech.E.

Sixth, letters indicating an appointment or office, such as M.P., Q.C., J.P., D.L., M.L.A., M.L.C. Where both J.P. and D.L. are used, J.P. should come before D.L., since a Justice of the Peace is appointed by the Sovereign, while a Deputy Lieutenant is appointed by the Lord

Lieutenant of the county. Neither of these affixes is used, however, unless writing on business connected with the appointment. Q.C. appears last of all lettering except M.P. (or its equivalent):

F. T. Martin, Esq., Q.C., M.P.

THE UNIVERSITIES

CHANCELLORS

In speech they are addressed formally as Sir or (in the case of a peer) My Lord or Your Grace as the case may be. More familiarly as Mr Chancellor or Chancellor.

In writing the most formal mode of address is:

Sir (or according to peerage rank),

> I am, Sir (My Lord),
>> Your obedient servant,

Less formally:

My Lord, *or*
Dear Sir,

> Yours faithfully,

The social manner is:

Dear Mr Chancellor, *or*
Dear Chancellor,

> Yours sincerely,

Address of envelope in both cases—
> The Rt. Hon. The Earl of Blank,
>> Chancellor of the University of ————.

VICE-CHANCELLORS

The rules as for CHANCELLORS apply (Dear Mr Vice-Chancellor, or Dear Vice-Chancellor, etc.) excepting that the envelope is addressed thus:

The Vice-Chancellor of The University of ————.

The two exceptions to this are Vice-Chancellors of Oxford and Cambridge, who are addressed respectively as:

The Revd. The Vice-Chancellor of The University of Oxford (whether or not he is in Holy Orders)

and

The Right Worshipful The Vice-Chancellor of The University of Cambridge.

The prefix is used only with the office, not with the individual's name.

See also Principals (p. 175).

HIGH STEWARDS

are addressed in speech according to their rank. In writing the most formal mode is:

Sir (or according to peerage rank),
> I am, Sir (My Lord),
>> Your obedient servant,

Less formally:

Dear Sir, *or*
My Lord,
> Yours faithfully,

The social manner is:

Dear High Steward,
> Yours sincerely,

Address of envelope in both cases—
> His Grace The Duke of Blank,
>> High Steward of The University of —————.

DEPUTY HIGH STEWARDS

As High Stewards.

HEADS OF COLLEGES

May be known as Masters, Mistresses, Presidents, Principals, Provosts, Rectors, or Wardens.

In speech they are addressed formally as Sir or Madam. Socially by name.

In writing they are addressed most formally as:

Sir (or Madam),
                    Your obedient servant,

Less formally:

Dear Sir (or Madam),
                    Yours faithfully,

Socially the address is:

Dear Master of ———— College.
Dear Mistress of ———— College.
Dear President of ———— College, etc.

or informally,

Dear Master.

Address of envelope in both cases—
                    The Master of ———— College, etc.

DEANS

of colleges are addressed according to their own name and rank. In the rare cases (cathedral colleges) where a dean is head he is a dean of the Church of England and must be addressed as such (*see* p. 120).

PRINCIPALS

The head of a Scottish University may be appointed Principal and Vice-Chancellor, and the heads of the Constituent Colleges of the University of Wales are known as Principals. They are addressed both in speech and in writing as Principal, under the same rules as a head of a college.

PROFESSORS

The title is used in speech and writing, formally and socially.

Most formally:

Dear Sir (or Madam),

> I am, dear Sir (or Madam),
>> Your obedient servant,

Less formally:

Dear Sir (or Madam),

>> Yours faithfully,

Socially:

Dear Professor Dash,

>> Yours sincerely,

Address of envelope in both cases—
>> Professor J. G. Dash.

ORDAINED PROFESSORS

An ordained professor is referred and spoken to in speech and writing as Professor Blank. He should be addressed on envelopes, both formally and socially, as The Revd. Professor W. L. Blank. If he is a Canon he is addressed as such (*see* p. 122). Such accumulations as Professor the Revd. Canon ————, though not unknown, are undesirable.

DEGREES

The custom established and used by the older universities is really the best to follow. The rule is that doctors in any faculty use the designation, while lower degrees (e.g. M.A., LL.B., B.Sc., etc.) are omitted, except in circumstances where *all* academic qualifications are appropriate. Even then only the higher of two degrees in the same faculty would be used. Outside academic circles even doctorates would not be appended to the name in a social letter, although of course anyone customarily known as Dr. ———— would still be so. It is a matter of individual choice whether the holder of a doctorate is addressed as Dr. ———— or as John ————, Esq., with the appropriate lettering, except that it is now the custom always to write the letters D.D. (*See also* Doctors of Medicine, p. 178). It is never correct to write Dr. ————, Ph.D. (or whatever the lettering might be).

DOCTORS

Degrees are given by the older and most of the newer universities in seven faculties: Divinity, Law, Literature, Medicine, Music, Philosophy and Science. The following are the various styles and abbreviations:

DOCTOR OF DIVINITY . D.D.

DOCTOR OF LAWS . LL.D.

       Conferred by Cambridge and all other universities granting degrees in this faculty.

DOCTOR OF CIVIL LAW . D.C.L.

       This is the Oxford, Durham and Newcastle upon Tyne degree corresponding to the Cambridge LL.D.

DOCTOR OF LITERATURE ⎫ Litt.D. (Cambridge, Dublin and
DOCTOR OF LETTERS ⎬   Liverpool.)
             ⎭ D.Litt. (Oxford and some others)

              D.Lit. (London and Manchester)

DOCTOR OF MEDICINE . M.D. (all universities except Oxford)

              D.M. (Oxford University)

DOCTOR OF MUSIC . Mus.D. (Cambridge and Durham)

              D.Mus. (Oxford)

DOCTOR OF PHILOSOPHY Ph.D. (Cambridge and others)

              D.Phil. (Oxford)

DOCTOR OF SCIENCE   .   Sc.D. (Cambridge and Dublin)
D.Sc. (Oxford and others)

DOCTORS OF MEDICINE

The title has become so wedded to the medical profession that the reminder is needed that not all qualified medical men hold the final degree. Those who do are addressed and referred to in speech as Dr. Gray, and letters are addressed:

Thomas Gray, Esq., M.D.

(but in Scotland more usually, Dr. Thomas Gray).

If a knighthood or baronetcy has been conferred, the address in speech becomes Sir Thomas Gray or Sir Thomas, and the envelope would be inscribed:

Sir Thomas Gray, M.D.,   *or*
Sir Thomas Gray, Bt., M.D.

If a peerage has been conferred the address in speech and writing is according to rank (*see* under appropriate headings) with perhaps the degree of medicine added after the more important honours.

Those medical men who have not taken the final degree are addressed in every way as if they have, excepting that their actual qualifications, such as M.B., L.R.C.P., would be substituted for M.D. on the envelope, or, as is normal with general practitioners, they are called simply Dr. —————.

There is also the firmly established custom in the medical profession of addressing surgeons both in speech and writing as Mr, and inscribing the envelope thus:

T. Gray, Esq., F.R.C.S.

Gynaecologists tend to be addressed as surgeons in England and Wales, as doctors elsewhere.

DOCTORS OF DIVINITY

are usually but not always clergymen. The degree can, in some Universities, be taken by, or conferred on, laymen as well. In the case of the clergy, they are addressed and referred to in speech as Dr. Read. Formal letters would begin Reverend Sir; social ones, Dear Dr. Read, and the envelope in each case would be addressed:

The Revd. J. L. Read, D.D.

HONORARY DOCTORATES

The same rules for use apply as to other holders, although it is not usual to add them if there are other letters after the name already, except in the most comprehensive lists; and they are of course not used in circumstances where they might seem to imply an academic qualification. Many holders of honorary doctorates do enjoy the use of the title Doctor, and their preference should be followed.

LESSER DEGREES

Letters denoting masters' and bachelors' degrees, which are, of course, most common, are not used even in university circles in ordinary correspondence, and socially they are not used at all. There are certain formal occasions on which members of learned professions would use them, such as in lists of lectures, etc., but a master's or bachelor's degree would not be appended to a doctor's. The reason for this is that in the older universities a doctor's degree is considered to include an M.A.—it can only very rarely be taken without it.

| MASTER OF ARTS | . | . | . | M.A. |
| BACHELOR OF ARTS | . | . | . | B.A. |

BACHELOR OF LETTERS .	.	. B.Litt.
BACHELOR OF DIVINITY.	.	. B.D.
MASTER OF LAWS .	.	. LL.M.
BACHELOR OF LAWS .	.	. LL.B.
BACHELOR OF CIVIL LAW	.	. B.C.L.
BACHELOR OF MEDICINE	.	. M.B.
BACHELOR OF MEDICINE	.	. B.M. (Oxford)
BACHELOR OF MUSIC .	.	. { B.Mus. / Mus.B. / Mus.Bac.
BACHELOR OF SCIENCE .	.	. B.Sc.

INDEX